W9-CMN-899

John Ford and the Caroline Theatre

John Ford and the Caroline Theatre

Dorothy M. Farr

BOOKS
10 East 53d St., New York 10022
(a division of Harper & Row Publishers, Inc.)

First published 1979 by
THE MACMILLAN PRESS LTD
London and Basingstoke
Published in the U.S.A. 1979 by
HARPER & ROW PUBLISHERS, INC.
BARNES & NOBLE IMPORT DIVISION

Printed in Great Britain

Library of Congress Cataloging in Publication Data

Farr, Dorothy Mary

  John Ford and the Caroline theatre.

  Bibliography: p.
  1. Ford, John, 1586-ca. 1640 — Stage history.

2. Ford, John, 1586-ca. 1640 — Criticism and
interpretation. 3. Theater — England — History.
I. Title.
PR2528.S75F3 1978   822′.3   78-12679
ISBN 0-06-492065-8

For Catherine

Contents

Notes on the Text   viii

Acknowledgements   ix

1 Poet-dramatist in the Caroline Theatre   1

2 *The Lover's Melancholy:*
   a play for Blackfriars   16

3 The Revenge Motive in *'Tis Pity She's a Whore:*
   a play for the Phoenix Theatre   36

4 Reassessment of the *Othello* theme at the Phoenix in
   Love's Sacrifice   58

5 Return to Blackfriars and the Classical Tragic
   Pattern in *The Broken Heart*   79

6 Revival of Chronicle History at the Phoenix in
   Perkin Warbeck   105

7 Return to Domestic Tragi-comedy at the Phoenix in
   The Lady's Trial and *The Fancies Chaste and Noble*   125

8 The Challenge of the Caroline Theatre   150

Appendix *The Queen* or *The Excellency of her Sex*   161

Notes   167

Select Bibliography   178

Index   181

Notes on the Text

Quotations from Ford's plays are as follows:

From *John Ford*, H. Havelock Ellis, Mermaid edition (1888)
The Lover's Melancholy
'Tis Pity She's a Whore
Love's Sacrifice
The Broken Heart
Perkin Warbeck

From *The Dramatic Works of John Ford*, ed. William Gifford, (1827)
The Fancies Chaste and Noble
The Lady's Trial

From W. Bang, *Materialen* (Louvain, 1906)
The Queen

Acknowledgements

I wish to express my gratitude to the Head of the Language and Literature Department of the Birmingham Central Library, and her staff, and also to the Librarian and staff of the Stourbridge District Library, for unfailing help over a period of reading and investigation which eventually led to the writing of this book.

I should also like to thank Dr Stanley Dixon for kindly aiding me in the reading of the proofs.

1 Poet-dramatist in the Caroline Theatre

John Ford stands between two worlds in the theatre of his time. His uniqueness, which has stimulated so much commentary over the past fifty years, lies primarily in his response as an artist to that situation. In date, in manner and attitude, to some extent in the content of his surviving independent plays, he is clearly of the Caroline theatre, but his habit of presenting Caroline conceptions within a Jacobean pattern, his obvious attachment to a drama which most of his contemporaries would regard as outworn, have placed him to the modern view as 'in every way a conclusion',[1] — in effect the last of the Jacobean poet-dramatists.

Ford's reputation is muddied with contradictory assumptions; Lamb's admiration and the fair assessments of Joan Sargeaunt[2] and Una Ellis-Fermor[3] have been countered by the opinions, often curiously prejudiced, of those who dismiss his work as part of the decadence,[4] nor is the general impression of Ford as a dramatist any clearer for those who find in him an exponent either of Burtonian psychology[5] or of the traditional moral order.[6] A recent tendency to approach Ford's plays as a matter for the study rather than the stage is an easy and totally misleading evasion of the problem. The cumulative effect has been to lend an air of elderliness and remoteness to one of the most enterprising and individual dramatists of the early seventeenth century theatre.

A partial explanation is that except in name nothing is known of Ford's independent plays before he reached the age of forty. But another, and more important, is a general lack of interest in the nature and use of the Caroline stage. Most students of drama know a good deal about the Elizabethan and Jacobean theatres; they know far less about those which functioned during the reign of Charles I. With our hindsight of what was to come we tend to regard both the stage and the drama of that period as a dead end, an appendage to the Jacobean era, providing temporary fare for an audience of tired interest and declining numbers.

1

Now while there is some truth in this conclusion it ignores the growing importance of the private theatres during the period and the impetus which the influence of the Sovereign and the Court was giving to new developments in drama — trends already felt in Jacobean years, for instance in Shakespeare's last plays and in the early work of Beaumont and Fletcher at Blackfriars and the Globe. After many readings of Ford's unaided plays I am convinced that they can be fully appreciated — in fact that we can know what Ford was about — only in the context of the two theatres for which they were intended. Five of the surviving independent plays were written for the Phoenix (earlier the Cockpit) in Drury Lane under Beeston's management, and probably performed by Queen Henrietta's Men,[7] and two for the King's Men at Blackfriars. As I try to show in succeeding chapters Ford seems to have thought and written with the shortcomings as well as the opportunities of his stage and his audience in mind, and this, considering his continuing association with one of the most important of the private theatres while maintaining an intermittent connection with the leading company of actors in London, suggests not the 'armchair dramatist' but the serious professional.

During the Caroline period the private — or rather enclosed, indoor — theatre became less the exception than the rule. Another tendency encouraged by the King and supported by the influence of the Queen and the Court was the exclusive use of the theatres for the performance of plays, instead of serving the dual purpose of popular entertainment such as cock-fighting, bear-baiting, fencing, as well as drama. The Blackfriars theatre in the old Blackfriars Priory and the Phoenix theatre in Drury Lane had both grown up in the Jacobean period. When in 1607/8 Henry Evans relinquished his lease for the Children's companies of part of the Blackfriars buildings, the King's Men took over the property with additional rooms as winter quarters which they retained until the closure of the theatres in 1642. But the Phoenix had been a good example of the dual-purpose theatre, for it was a reconstruction of the old Cockpit, now owned by Christopher Beeston, a colleague of Shakespeare. In 1616 Beeston converted the Cockpit into a private theatre, exclusively for stage plays, and renamed it the 'Phoenix', although it continued to be known popularly and perhaps affectionately as the Cockpit. A third private theatre was Salisbury Court, built in Fleet Street in 1629. When a little later King Charles commissioned Inigo Jones to reconstruct the Cockpit-in-Court, which had been a dual-purpose playhouse occupying the site of the present No. 10 Downing Street, as a theatre for the exclusive use of players he did the theatre a lasting service by example; but as far as drama itself was concerned this trend backed by royal influence was not immediately an unmixed blessing. Although the Globe catered only for playgoers, those who frequented other playhouses, in the sense of 'game houses', for cock-fighting or fencing might come again to see a play. The banishment of popular sports from the theatre at this time may have contributed to the decline of the popular audience and the split between the private and popular theatres. However necessary to theatrical standards it facilitated a sophistication which any poet-dramatist had to reckon with.

More is known about the Blackfriars Theatre[8] in Ford's day than about the Phoenix. At the former the auditorium was rectangular, measuring approximately 66ft by 46ft, with the stage projecting from one of the shorter walls. The audience capacity was about 700 as against between 2000 and 3000 at the Globe, but as was customary in the indoor theatres the spectators were all seated, with a few stools on the stage itself. Two doors opening behind the stage to other quarters were used for entrances and there may have been another entrance on either side to allow for passing over the stage[9] or for processions and general mobility. The actors' tiring house was probably behind the stage front and an upper room with one or two windows overlooking the stage may have been used for this purpose, but there is little evidence in plays written primarily for this theatre that an upper acting level was often called for. It is however quite possible that a movable booth with hangings and a strongly constructed canopy which could function as an upper stage could be brought in when required. Since musical interludes were traditional at Blackfriars there must have been some provision for musicians. The boxes which flanked the stage were probably for the use of spectators, but according to Alfred Harbage the theatre was lofty enough to allow for galleries.[10] It is possible therefore that either a musicians' gallery existed over the stage end or it was built out from the tiring house as was the case in the reconstructed Cockpit-in-Court.

Lighting was by torches and hanging candelabra. As we know from some of Ben Jonson's later Inductions lights needed trimming between the Acts;[11] this applied particularly to torches, which were apt to smoke so badly that the King went to the expense of a new 'mask-house' at Whitehall to preserve the Reubens painting in the banqueting hall where masques were previously performed at Court. Fire risk must have been acute; on the other hand the staging of masques demanding ingenious placing of torches, and lighting effects by the use of candles behind tinted glass, inevitably set a standard for performances in the private theatres, so that professional skill in the lighting of plays was on the up-grade. One result of artificial lighting was the effective staging and consequent frequency of scenes in darkness or half-light. Davenant's *The Wits*, a slow play in itself, rises to a climax in later scenes which take place in a crypt with 'an iron crow' and a 'dark lanthorn'.

But it was at the Phoenix that Ford found his home as an artist. This theatre was probably, like most cockpits or bear pits, circular or octagonal in shape and perhaps about 50ft in diameter. The original pillars supporting the roof and the galleries surrounding the cockpit were probably put to use, making a stage front with a balcony or upper stage[12] opening out of the tiring room. There were at least three doors at the back of the lower stage and perhaps another on either side, and a movable booth, similar to that at Blackfriars with its useful upper stage level, was probably available.[13] Stage directions suggest that both at the Phoenix and at Blackfriars curtains or hangings stretching across the entire stage, opening and closing to their entire extent, were a permanent feature for discoveries or exits and entrances as well as for scene changing.

On such a stage with a small intimate audience at close quarters, while stage management was simpler, flexibility was imperative. In the larger open theatres such as the Globe, the Fortune and the Swan, a number of scene changes were possible, for the size of the stage allowed for division into various localities. Here in the small indoor theatres the tendency was to envisage an open space — a hall or town square — as common ground where a good deal of the action could take place. The elaborate or bulky stage properties familiar in the Jacobean open theatre would be unusable here, nor was there much scope for battle scenes or spectacular martial array. Yet spectacle there certainly was, if on a smaller scale. Costumes had to be lavish for they were to be seen attractively lighted and at short range; precision of hand and foot movement was demanded for the same reason. Spectacle was a natural requirement for an audience who knew all about the masques at Court and in noble houses whether they had witnessed an actual performance or not, and the incidence of short masques and formal dances evidently added to a play's box-office value. But all this required formal but comparatively restricted grouping, often in an emblematic manner, or round some object — a tomb, an altar or a banquet — of emblematic significance, rather than a pageant or crowd scene. Colourful hangings, painted and gilded surrounds and backgrounds would be a necessity, and when the company could afford it a good deal of scenery in the form of backcloths and three-dimensional objects was probably used. But these were theatres designed for listening as well as for scenic display. Ford's complaint in the Prologue to *The Lover's Melancholy* that poetry was becoming 'a trade' at least indicates that there were those in his audience who understood what he meant and also knew how to listen to good poetry when they heard it in the theatre. As we shall see later Ford was to use the acoustical amenities of the intimate theatre to great advantage.

Admission prices ranging from sixpence to about eighteen pence to two shillings or even half a crown,[14] must have conditioned the social and cultural level of the audience to some extent. Jonson had some double-edged remarks about the 'sinful sixpenny mechanics' who occupied seats in 'the oblique caves and wedges of your house' at Blackfriars.[15] But if he poked a little fun at those who strained their resources to be up to date however uncomfortable the seating, he despised still more the 'plush and velvet outsides ... of clothes not understanding' of their social betters. Only the prosperous could afford to frequent the private theatres and the dramatists' habit of referring to and quoting from other plays in the repertoire suggests that they were catering for habitués.

In fact in the Caroline as in the later Jacobean theatre there was
something analogous to the modern theatre club — intimate,
social, urbane — but it was also a place where people came to
be seen as well as to see!

It is easy to think of the Caroline public as living uneasily
under the shadow of impending civil war and the theatre as a
means of escape. In fact, as Petegorsky remarks[16] the reverse
was probably the case. Taxation was increasingly burdensome
and there were ominous bickerings between King and
Parliament; demands for Ship Money and the King's backing
of Archbishop Laud's high-handed ecclesiastical policy were
recurring sources of discontent. Yet as David Matthew's
background study makes abundantly clear, in the country at
large the period was one of peaceful and quiet establishment
such as had not been known for generations.[17]

On the whole the middle classes were comfortable and there
seemed no lack of money either in the royal household or in
the pockets of merchants and businessmen. The shipping on
the Thames in contemporary engravings was an image of a
superficial prosperity. Although at the expense of some native
industries foreign trade was developing, and if the rural
labouring population was becoming poorer, to the fortunate
the period may well have seemed one of 'prosperity and ad-
ministrative efficiency'[18] and those who could afford elegant
pleasures could also afford to be oblivious to the growing
menace of Puritan resistance. The King was an assiduous
patron of the arts; he had bought and commissioned many
paintings by Van Dyck and Reubens for Whitehall, Inigo
Jones was constantly called upon to design not only stage sets
for masques but also royal palaces, for instance the Queen's
House at Greenwich and additions to the palace at Whitehall.
Charles's interest in plays such as those of William Cartwright,
whose high-minded idealism was combined with a fine lyrical
gift, and his evident preference for single-purpose playhouses,
suggest a determination to raise the moral and artistic level of
stage plays. This was the royal answer to Puritan criticism of
the Queen's obsessive pursuit of theatrical entertainment in
her own circle. Charles had continued the Jacobean policy of
bringing leading companies of actors under royal patronage
and now all the London companies were under the patronage
of members of the royal family. It was inevitable that players
should hope for an invitation to perform at Court and that

they should therefore bear in mind the taste of the King or Queen and the leading courtiers in the plays they presented and in their manner of staging them. Neither the private nor the public theatres could escape this trend away from the popular and the general to the sophisticated and the select.

No doubt for widely different reasons both actors and audiences began to demand what was new and fashionable, and as fashion is fickle so were Caroline tastes in drama. The Queen and her ladies had fostered an etiolated Platonic idealism which, expressed in the music and dancing of the masque and in drama based on pseudo-classical romances, could titillate the imagination with a moral sententiousness. Certain themes recur — heroic love, friendship, constancy in love and in marriage, the never-exhausted topic of honour; all these seem to have their phases of popularity, decline and revival according to audience reaction and demand. The more complicated the intrigue the greater the interest; surprise endings, spectacular climaxes and an abundance of disguises were necessary to keep the theatre alert. Nevertheless Clifford Leech's comment that the private audience 'strayed from an idea'[19] is open to question. These were theatres whose shape and dimensions lent themselves to casuistical argument. Instances of serious and sustained dialogue are to be found in tragedy and tragi-comedy, and in particular in the plays of Ford and Massinger, and it was in the private theatres that the new interest in psychological states fostered by the publication of Burton's *Anatomy of Melancholy* in 1621 made an appeal which led to an analytical if stereotyped approach to character.

The problem for the dramatist was that while none of these interests ran deep, few persisted. In this theatre there was no place for popular tradition, none for the daily goings-on of the people of London who had been the backbone of the audience during Shakespeare's best years at the Globe. Historical plays and realistic domestic drama were rare and tragedy which plumbed the depths of human experience through the motives of jealousy or revenge or through the deeper passions was out of date. On the other hand satirical comedy, wit and raillery, with a good spice of bawdry, provided it kept within the bounds of apparent decency, were popular. The general outlook was aristocratic, superficially refined and often unreal.

For the poet-dramatist a persistent subject of complaint was the decline of dramatic poetry in the theatre. In the Prologue to *The Lady's Trial* Theophilus Bird, who perhaps both wrote and spoke it, protests on Ford's behalf that 'The muses chatter who were wont to sing'; and Ford himself in the Prologue to *The Broken Heart* (assuming that this prologue can be attributed to him) cavils at the public taste for satire — 'some lame jeer At place or persons' — which seriously limited the poet's art. Yet the dramatist's position in the private theatre, though less independent than in the days of the Children's companies, was more secure than in the public theatre, and there was always the possibility of catching the notice of influential persons about the Court. For professional playwrights a new source of irritation was the advent of the amateurs — poets often of means or social standing trying their hand at the stage. Such were, among others, Suckling, Killigrew and Cartwright. For the amateurs play-writing was a fashionable pastime; their plays might be produced at Court if they were lucky or at an Inn of Court or in the private theatres. Suckling's *Aglaura* was a byword for its lavish staging and the climax of Cartwright's *The Royal Slave* would require some kind of transformation scene more suited to a masque. These were poets whose contribution to the drama has come down to us, but in his comedy *The Antipodes* Brome has some rough handling for the new nobility imitating the Court by providing ostentatious dramatic entertainment in their own houses in the figure of Lord Letoy. Letoy boasts of maintaining his own actors, his own music and of writing his own plays — 'all within myself' — after which 'many servitors, richly apparelled' pass over the stage 'doing honour to Letoy as they pass'.[20] Yet in spite of its limitations and frustrations professional playwrights evidently believed their prospects in the private theatre were sound and it was to this theatre that Ford turned when he relinquished the traditional occupation of a legal family for the stage.

John Ford was born at Islington in Devon in 1586. He entered the Middle Temple in 1602, no doubt with the intention of following a legal profession. But writing had been an interest at an early age and although his non-dramatic works fall outside the purpose of this book, some of them were indicative of the kind of dramatist he came to be. The constructively critical spirit which enlivens his characteristic plays may have inspired *Fame's Memorial* of 1606, an elegiac poem occasioned by the death of Lord Mountjoy, who had flown in the face of public opinion by marrying illegally Penelope, Sidney's 'Stella', after her divorce from Lord Rich by an ecclesiastical process debarring remarriage. The unhappiness of Penelope's marriage with Rich and her liaison with Mountjoy were common knowledge.[21] This was the Ford who would present with understanding and balance the plight of a pair of lovers in an incestuous relationship in *'Tis Pity She's a Whore* and give a sympathetic account of the imposture of Perkin Warbeck in the play of that name without distorting the facts of history. *Honour Triumphant*, a prose work also published in 1606, is again of interest here as representing the young Ford's impressions of the dominant ideas and ideals of his time. This attempt at sophistication by a young writer seeking recognition[22] nevertheless contains in embryo the ideas of a coterie which he was to humour for artistic purposes of his own in mature work for the theatre.

Ford was writing for the old Cockpit as early as 1613 when a lost play attributed to him, *An Ill Beginning has a Good End*, was performed there by Queen Anne's Men. Other plays followed of which only the names remain. Two comedies, *The London Merchant* and *The Royal Combat*, and a tragedy, *Beauty in a Trance*, were his in their entirety; unfortunately we have no means of dating them. Somewhere in this decade Ford probably wrote *The Queen* or *The Excellency of her Sex. The Queen* was published anonymously in 1653 but is now generally accepted as Ford's work. As the play is markedly inferior in quality to Ford's other surviving work and is difficult to place in the Ford canon, I have dealt with it in an appendix. Its interest here is its suitability in many respects to the taste of a Caroline audience and in what it suggests of a young writer's reaction to current trends.

As the subtitle indicates the Queen is presented as the ideal of womanhood — in this case of wifehood — on a heroic and romantic level. The Queen's Griselda-like patience and loving submission when Alphonso, whose rebellion she had pardoned to the extent of making him her consort and King, refuses to live with her after their marriage and subsequently accuses her of unfaithfulness — all this, combined with her beauty which he is constrained to acknowledge, was familiar

material from the courtly romances of D'Urfé. It also recalls
the tragi-comedies of Beaumont and Fletcher. Again, in the
forgiveness which helps to overcome Alphonso's dislike of her
sex and her refusal to jeopardise her subject's lives by allowing
them to champion her cause, she also presents the power of
love and the demands of honour. The theme of honour recurs
in the sub-plot, in Velasco's obdurate determination to stand
by the oath he has made to Salassa not to fight in any cause,
notwithstanding her willingness to release him from it. Apart
from the qualities they represent the characters are pasteboard
cut-outs. Yet there is plenty of incident, a good deal of
opportunity for elaborate staging and lavish costume, and
certainly no lack of surprises. Three times a public execution
with the usual macabre panoply of the scaffold on stage is
interrupted by a last-minute reprieve, three times a champion is
summoned at the sound of a trumpet and martial figures form
up and move across the stage; the plot with its equally eventful
sub-plot is constructed with the maximum amount of intrigue
and complexity. All this would be colourful enough in a small
acting space but it could be easily transferred to a larger one,
and since in those of his plays which can be dated
approximately Ford never moved from the private theatre the
play may well have been written for the King's Men at
Blackfriars and subsequently at the Globe. If so *The Queen*
may be some indication of the way in which Ford was looking
at the problems of his theatre. Obviously he was feeling his
way, earnestly studying the inclination of his audience by
providing all they were likely to want in a single play. That the
play falls below the standard of his other earlier work may be
some evidence that he was trying too hard!

Ford may have been testing his skill in these early plays but
he was certainly not idle and that he was regarded as a coming
dramatist may explain his collaboration with Dekker and
other established playwrights between 1612 and 1625. Two
lost plays — *The Bristowe Merchant* and *The Fairy Knight* —
were written with Dekker and in 1621 *The Witch of Edmonton*
by Dekker, Ford, Rowley and others was presented at
Whitehall and later acted at the Phoenix. Ford also
collaborated with Dekker in *The Sun's Darling*, another
Phoenix play, in 1624, and probably with Rowley in *The
Spanish Gipsy* in 1623.

At about this time Ford had a brief partnership with Webster. *A Fair Maid of the Inn* by Massinger, Webster and Ford was written about 1625 and was possibly acted at Blackfriars or the Phoenix.[23] Another lost play one would like to have known was *The Late Murder of the Son Upon the Mother* by Webster and Ford. Of this probably true story only a scurrilous ballad — *Keep the Widow Waking* — survives.

As Ford's plays are notoriously difficult to date no phases of development can be defined, but it is tempting to see in these years of collaboration a preliminary to the great period of his authentic independent work between, approximately, 1628 and 1638. We have only to read the probable Ford scenes in *The Witch of Edmonton* and *The Spanish Gipsy*[24] to be aware of something strongly individual, a purpose which, if his hand has been rightly discerned, was forming in these early years and would carry him forward to an achievement which he had probably set himself.

Ford earned a certain notoriety in writing what was probably the first of his mature plays in their entirety, after Burton. This was *The Lover's Melancholy*,[25] licensed in 1628 and acted by the King's Men at Blackfriars and the Globe. A whole scene is devoted to a masque presenting various types of melancholy in order to focus attention on love melancholy. Ford is careful to acknowledge his debt to *The Anatomy of Melancholy* in a marginal note in the text.

The choice of subject was a wise one, for Burton had caught the public fancy and his theories, some of which still hold good, were beginning to condition contemporary psychology. To some extent the play is a statement of intention in further work, for while it demonstrates the causes and cure of mental illness it is also a first study in the application of the psychological method to the conception of character. Here too are Ford's first clear borrowings from Shakespeare and Beaumont and Fletcher, first essays in a habit he was to make part of his craftsman's practice in plays to come. *The Lover's Melancholy* is an interesting pastiche of old and new, and if we can clear our minds of Platonic idealism and Burtonian formulae, it is an arresting experiment in dramatic art.[26] Unfortunately the play seems to have stamped Ford's work in the public eye both in his own day and ours. But the debt to Burton need not imply that he saw the behaviour of his characters, even in this play, entirely in the light of Burton's theories or that the *Anatomy* was of greater importance than any other influence. It was merely topical.

There followed three plays written in their several ways to the pattern of what may be loosely called Revenge Tragedy, all published in 1633. *'Tis Pity She's a Whore*, acted by the Queen's Men at the Phoenix theatre, is a daring restatement of the revenge motive in the context of an abnormal situation. *Love's Sacrifice*, also a Phoenix play, in which Ford revived and reshaped the 'Othello' theme, probably followed, for both in style and content it shows clear associations with *'Tis Pity*. Last of the three tragedies in this group was probably *The Broken Heart*, written for the King's Men at Blackfriars.[27] In this, perhaps Ford's greatest, certainly his most poetic play, he revived the classical tragic form and tried to reconcile it with the Jacobean revenge motive and Caroline conceptions of love and honour.

From these three tragedies modelled on established dramatic patterns Ford now turned to chronicle history in the tragedy of *Perkin Warbeck*, again acted at the Phoenix theatre and published in 1634[28] — a type of play which he himself describes in the Prologue as 'out of fashion', an old form with a new content and with Ford's characteristic stamp. This was to be his last tragedy for after this he turned, again backwards, to the domestic drama which had been popular some years earlier in the plays of Dekker and Heywood. First probably came *The Fancies Chaste and Noble*,[29] a tragi-comedy in which the main plot offers some problems. The sub-plot however is built upon a domestic situation which looks back to the Winefred scenes in *The Witch of Edmonton*. The play was printed in 1638 together with *The Lady's Trial*, a domestic tragi-comedy and one of Ford's most interesting experiments, which was acted at the Phoenix in the same year.

This constant return to traditional forms of drama has met with a good deal of criticism; so also has his persistent borrowing in these plays from the work of other dramatists. Ford's purpose in thus taking up and rethinking one dramatic pattern after another has received less attention. Miss Bradbrook dismissed his use of the older conventions as 'passive'.[30] On the other hand Professor Oliver believes that he was seeking a new medium and failing because he could not 'shake off the shackles of Jacobean drama'.[31]

I cannot agree with either of these comments. In every case the pattern of the play, the shape of the plot and the central situation are familiar, but Ford never fails to surprise us with what he makes of the old medium, the borrowed character or concept. Ford is a far from 'passive' imitator. Nor, I think, was he seeking a new medium; had this been his intention more radical innovations in dramatic form might have been expected, or a repetition of successful experiments, instead of passing from one type of drama to another.

This is a problem which should be considered within the context of the Blackfriars and the Phoenix theatres and against the struggle to please a difficult audience without debasing art. Jonson exposed his resistance to the age in the bitter raillery of his later satires, Massinger produced a wealth of tragi-comedy in which a compromise with a taste not his own is often discernible, Brome, Shirley and Davenant built up a body of social and witty comedy; few stage poets ventured upon tragedy. It is the more significant then that of these seven plays of Ford four are tragedies and of the three tragi-comedies only one owes anything to romance. Ford appears to have been seeking for fresh relevances in dramatic themes and patterns which had stood the test in the Elizabethan and Jacobean theatres, so that by thinking through them he might come to terms with the new impetus which he saw emerging in ideas, in moral standpoints and in attitudes to human character, viewpoints which for better or worse would make for changes in the contemporary theatre.

In considering Ford's dramatic work as a whole an unavoidable impression is that of a persistent purpose, evolving in some of his early collaboration to find fullest expression in his mature and independent plays. In all this work, especially in the tragedies, we meet the recurring question why men and women behave as they do and find the answer not in society, not in pressures from without but in tensions within the personality. The action is in the mind of the characters; physical encounters, though placed with care and economy and with an expert eye to the uses of the stage, are of ancillary importance to the theme. Ford had set himself a task which demanded ruthless selection; presentation of manners could only obstruct what he wanted to do, low comedy, even if he had had the skill for it, was no part of his purpose, though he made some concessions to public demand for comic relief. So we find a concentration upon a kind of social mean which Ford evidently found in sophisticated people. This was more than a concession to his audience, for it was at this social level that he found the human character relatively untrammelled by circumstances outside the scope of his intention. The Prince's Court is a useful symbolic background, but until *Perkin Warbeck* it has little relation to a real royal court. That of Palador in Cyprus is a small entity tightly knit, that of Amyclas in Sparta is a family rather than a courtly circle, that of Duke Caraffa is riddled with family rather than diplomatic contention. In all these plays the atmosphere is rather that of a typical great house. But the focus is narrowed; we see the characters only in the crises of their lives which, because they affect the personality at depth are bound to be emotional, and there is a deliberate reticence on many aspects of human intercourse which often enliven serious drama. In all this Ford seems to reassess the established patterns for a new psychological drama which, in this hybrid form, might preserve the best of the Jacobean achievement against the unpredictable situation in the Caroline theatre.

This is Ford's general aim, but associated with it and running through all the plays, however varied, is a theme which most of Ford's commentators have noted — that of constancy, a sort of integrity, not only on conduct but also and more importantly in character. The characters may strive to preserve this loyalty to the self against social and ethical laws as in *'Tis Pity*, or they may learn it under the discipline of a partly self-made situation as in *The Broken Heart* or *The Lady's Trial*, or they may attain it either by setting right or by facing the consequences of a wrong done in the past, as in *The Lover's Melancholy* or again in *The Broken Heart*. It is an equilibrium within the personality which Ford saw perhaps as typifying a basic need in the society of his day, but it was more than a pointer to a way of living, it was rather a suggestion for a means of survival.

In the following chapters I have tried to trace Ford's experimentation with traditional forms and to explore its functional importance in each play in itself, as well as its contribution to the Caroline dramatic vintage. I have also briefly considered Ford's handling of the stage in each play and his use of what the contemporary theatre had to offer. The plays are dealt with in the order in which I believe they are most likely to have appeared.

The plays of John Ford require many readings before they yield up the fullness of their quality. No one else in the period was quite like Ford. He has been compared with dramatists of the French classical school — with Corneille and Racine — but ultimately there is no satisfactory parallel. We are simply left where we began, with the uniqueness of Ford and the fascination of the problems which that uniqueness presents.

2 *The Lover's Melancholy*: a Play for Blackfriars

However it may sound to modern ears the title of this play was calculated to attract a Caroline private theatre audience. At Blackfriars in particular the hint of lovers' trials might suggest the romantic tragi-comedies, such as those of Beaumont and Fletcher and the later plays of Shakespeare, which had been popular in that theatre and were not yet forgotten, and whether they had read it or not, Ford could count upon the greater part of the audience at least having heard of *The Anatomy of Melancholy*. Although love melancholy is an initial interest the play is clearly built on recollections of two plays which may have been still in the repertory of the King's Men — *Philaster* of Beaumont and Fletcher, which provides the framework of the main plot, and *King Lear*, deliberately recalled in the tragic sub-plot. What Ford intended to make of his borrowings would in either case differ fundamentally from their source, but the affinity with *Philaster* is worth examining in detail for his clear departure from it.

Philaster is the dispossessed heir to the throne of Sicily, kept at the Court of the usurper to please the people. He is in love with Arethusa, daughter of the usurping King, who intends her for a Spanish prince, but Arethusa determines to follow her own inclination and gives Philaster to understand that he is her choice. Philaster thereupon places with her as go-between his page Bellario whom he has found and befriended in distress. Bellario is in fact a girl, daughter of a lord at the Court, who for love of Philaster has assumed this disguise in order to be near him. Malicious tongues cast suspicion on Arethusa's relations with Bellario and when Philaster accuses them both Bellario flies from his anger to the forest where later Philaster goes in distraction. When Arethusa strays from her father's hunting party all three meet.On the King's discovery of them Bellario convinces Philaster of her innocence by taking the blame for the wounds which he has inflicted in frenzy on herself and Arethusa. Afterwards while she and the Prince are in the custody of Arethusa at the palace she helps to reconcile the lovers, playing the part of Hymen at their secret marriage. Meantime a revolution rids the kingdom of the Spanish prince and sets Philaster in his rightful place. Whereupon the usurper repents and Bellario, her sex now revealed, remains to be the devoted handmaid of the Princess.

If Ford was using this play to attract the audience at Blackfriars he stripped the plot of political and, as far as possible, of romantic interest. Palador is the reigning Prince of Cyprus but he is seen against the background, not of a disturbed state, but of a circle of family connections and their friends in the Court. Like Philaster and like Hamlet, whom both heroes superficially resemble, he has had to bear the burden of a wrong done in the past, but Palador's hurt is of a deep personal nature touching neither his status nor his safety. His betrothal to Eroclea has been frustrated by his father Agenor, who, hoping to use her for his own pleasure, had confined her father Meleander and her younger sister Cleophila in the castle. We learn that Sophronos, Meleander's brother, protected her by effecting her escape disguised as a ship's boy. Under the name of Parthenophil, Eroclea has remained in this disguise, returning to Cyprus only after Agenor's death. Like Bellario she is found, still disguised, by Menaphon, the friend of the Prince's cousin Amethus and suitor to the latter's sister Thamasta, and like Bellario she is appointed as a page at Court. But whereas Bellario's adventures are of a primarily romantic interest, Parthenophil is in flight from dishonour; her continued disguise is not a device to satisfy a passion but a means of protection against a problematic situation in Cyprus. Although Ford has selected from his source those elements which will capture the interest of an audience familiar with romance, the concern of the play is with human fundamentals. Palador is overwhelmed with a melancholy which paralyses his will, Meleander, now crazed with grief, is anguished by the remembrance of past evil. Meantime, revealed now to Rhetias who has secretly aided Eroclea's return, Palador cherishes his lost love, and Meleander, tended only by Cleophila, remains out of sight and mind in his prison.

This is the core of the plot; what follows concerns the

diagnosis of Palador's sickness and that of Meleander and the cure of both. There is no attempt here to depict the ideal heroic prince or to surround him with an aura of romantic love. Parthenophil returns not to soothe her star-crossed lover but to claim her own right to him and to restore her father's reason. If in *Philaster* Bellario is the healer and reconciler she plays her part largely through the emotions. Here the whole action is therapeutic, for it turns increasingly upon the devices of Corax the physician, who is partnered in his work of healing by the honest and sharp-tongued Rhetias. In order to ascertain the cause of Palador's melancholy he stages a masque of melancholy in which, on the basis of Burton's theories, the various types of melancholy are presented. It is a scene not less spectacular in its way than the masque of the seven deadly sins in Marlowe's *Doctor Faustus*, but the approach is clinical and severely objective. There is however a gap in the list of characters which Palador queries; this, Corax explains, is for Love Melancholy, which art cannot present, and when he attempts to explain it the Prince abruptly terminates the episode. Corax is persuaded, and so presumably are the audience, that frustrated love is the cause of Palador's disorder, but Palador himself has been awakened from his lethargy to a sharp awareness of his need of Eroclea. This is the first of a series of awakenings on which the action is built.

Towards the close of the scene Corax refers — and is snubbed for doing so — to Thamasta's relations with Parthenophil in the secondary sub-plot. Like Arethusa in *Philaster* Thamasta has a proud independent spirit. She appears to be in some rebellion against her brother's sponsorship of Menaphon's suit and in this state she falls in love with Parthenophil, a situation no less unreal than the supposed love relationship between Arethusa and Bellario. In a delightful passage of dialogue after a scene of desperate wooing, Parthenophil reveals her sex; Thamasta recovers her balance but keeps the secret although she has to face rebuke from Amethus and Menaphon. Thamasta is also profiting from a kind of therapy — she is learning humility. Meanwhile in a scene of great beauty which will be dealt with later, Eroclea reveals herself to Palador, whose reaction, after the final impact of incredulous joy, is to come to himself and his duty as a just Prince.

We have already seen a good deal of the distracted Meleander and the ministrations of his daughter Cleophila whom Amethus hopes to marry. But Palador's meeting with him is rightly postponed until the Prince is himself in a fit state of mental health to make the resolutions and the reinstatement of Meleander, of the last act. In effect the Prince becomes the healer of the man his father has almost destroyed, and this under the professional eye of Corax, whose last 'cordial' is the restoration of Eroclea in an episode which recalls that of Cordelia to King Lear. So the characters come to themselves and their own peace by dealing justly and forgiving. The play has its weak, its unreal moments but it is a serious study in the needs, the risks and the greatness of the human spirit; no responsible critic would deny the play's faults, but of its kind and in its own way it is close-knit, sensitively conceived and precisely planned.

Nothing could more clearly distinguish Ford's method from that of Beaumont and Fletcher than their respective first impressions of Parthenophil and Bellario in the early scenes of either play. Bellario, innocent, untouched and unspoilt, concentrates like a child on her own grief and again like a child expresses it in terms of tenderness and the simple wisdom of the unsophisticated. Bellario's garland which Philaster finds her weaving is invested with the significance of country flower lore. The garland is an emblem of grief and is meant to appeal to the gentler emotions, as in Philaster's comment:

Seeing such pretty helpless innocence
Dwell in his face I asked him all his story.

I.2. p. 118 (Mermaid Edition)

And later Bellario will play with greater delicacy on the feelings of Philaster and Arethusa. Ultimately it is this hopeless but selfless love, making of itself a gift and an adorning, that sets Philaster on the way to harmony within, in order to face with humour and good sense the corruption he has fled from.[1] But Bellario has no real built-in dramatic function, nor is she emphatic enough to be a chorus character; she is simply an emotional accompaniment.

Now Ford is often charged with wringing the feelings but he is incapable of separating emotional appeal from dramatic content. There is a similar touch of folk tale and, at first sight, a not dissimilar appeal in Parthenophil's first appearance as described by Menaphon. He finds her playing with 'ravishing' skill upon the lute. The birds hover round to listen and the nightingale takes up the challenge; it is the contest of nature with art. But in contrast to Bellario, Parthenophil is a serious artist, performing not to ease her heart but for pure love of excellence 'whom study Had busied many hours to perfect practice ...

Upon his instrument he plays so swiftly...
That there was curiosity and cunning,
Concord and discord, lines of differing method
Meeting in one full centre of delight.

                                                    (I.1:p.12)

The whole episode is in itself a passage of music, but the real significance is in the ending. When the nightingale breaks its heart and falls dead upon the lute Parthenophil weeps for the bird, and her consequent attempt to destroy the instrument questions the validity of art as opposed to the best that nature can do.[2] Menaphon intervenes to spare the lute but both characters will learn that nature can never yield of its best unless controlled by the human spirit.

The Bellario episode is introductory and explanatory of her contribution to the action, but Parthenophil's musical contest points to the core of Ford's play. Throughout Parthenophil has the artist's eye for the right action and the right moment; when, still in disguise, she sees her father and shares his mental anguish, she will not anticipate her entrance in her own shape nor, though she shows signs of deep distress, will she voice it — in asides or in cryptic speech — before the time. What Corax, the other artist in the play, does professionally, Parthenophil in her relations with other characters does humanly. Her business is not to stimulate the feelings but to channel and control them. Inevitably emotional associations grow up round her but they are reflected in surrounding characters rather than expressed by herself. In contrast to the presentation of Bellario, Ford's handling of the character has a severe economy.

There is a similar selectiveness in the treatment of the amorous Princess and the jealous waiting-woman. In *Philaster* Megra, the lady-in-waiting, stages a piece of palace intrigue in order to accuse the innocent Arethusa; here it is the waiting-woman Kala who is unfairly accused and the Princess Thamasta who is guilty. Both underlings are bent upon mischief, but whereas Kala's action in informing Menaphon of Thamasta's relations with Parthenophil is a perfectly natural build-up of backstairs, not undeserved resentment, the whole conception of Megra in *Philaster* is intentionally obscene. Ford takes from it merely its usefulness as a device to expose the great lady to richly deserved rebuke, which in view of Parthenophil's sex turns to shame.

The conception of Thamasta carries the art/nature theme a stage further. Thamasta's sophistication is carefully stressed. Until the last Act she never forgets her privileged rank; her beauty is enhanced by 'helps of art', and attention is drawn to her garden — 'a pleasantly contrived delight' (I.3:p. 21). But in contrast to other characters she conceals behind all this a nature as yet untamed. The breeding of the princess is a thin covering to the passions and instincts of a magnificent animal; even to herself she is a 'lioness'. Her scorn of Menaphon's suit is part of a natural resistance to her brother's attempts to control her, and desire for Parthenophil, of which her training makes her ashamed, drives her to the naïve expedient of setting Kala to woo him for her — and into the equally naïve display of anger when her plan fails. But the discovery of her own folly in pursuing Parthenophil, the necessity of keeping silence under the reproaches of Amethus and Menaphon, and her generous admission of guilt are first steps in self-knowledge and self-control — 'I am sure awaked ... paid in my own coin.' Her next step is to communicate to Cleophila her repentance for her opposition, on grounds of her inferior birth, to the latter's betrothal to her brother Amethus.

Logically this sudden change of front may seem unreal, but the careful spacing of the Thamasta episodes and the witholding of her real intention until the final act, even the use of the foolish courtier Cucculus as messenger, combine to give the impression of a lapse of time and possible maturing of

purpose. Nor has the proud princess become a Griselda
overnight. When during her conversation with Cleophila she
hears Amethus and Menaphon imperiously demanding
entrance, it is the old Thamasta who turns upon them with —
'Must! Who are they say "must"? You are unmannerly'
(V.1:p.78). There is a touch of delicate humour in the
treatment of Thamasta but her development and the contrast
she presents to Eroclea and Cleophila contribute a good deal
to the association in this play of the function of art with the
training of the individual in cultivated society.

In all this Ford was deliberately restating the familiar story,
still popular in the Caroline theatre, of the true lovers
separated by an evil act or by irreversible circumstances in the
past and led through their trials by some healing influence.
Ford's theme is the ordering of disorder, not in circumstances
alone nor even in the moral health of the characters, but in the
personality itself. The story of Thamasta serves the play in
enlarging its scope beyond the limits of its title; love
melancholy is not in itself the subject of the play but rather a
symptom of a deeper malaise. The main characters are divided
against themselves and the purpose of the whole action is the
satisfaction of their basic need for an inner harmony, a
'concord in discord' of disparate yet complementary human
elements. Of this situation the State of Cyprus provides an
allegorical parallel rather than a background. Ford never
obtrudes an allegorical concept upon us but he often thinks
allegorically and there are indications that he was so thinking
here. Eroclea (true love) and Cleophila (lover of truth) are
meant to project moral qualities although Eroclea is none the
less a character in her own right. It is while both sisters are
absent from the Court that Rhetias refers to

> the madness of the times.....
> When commonwealths
Totter and reel from that nobility
And ancient virtue which renowns the great.

> (I.2:p.14)

The State of Cyprus is at variance with itself; its Prince is sick
in mind, the old nobleman Meleander mad, the courtiers
uneasy and the subjects critical of their ruler. Yet we have no
incipient rebellion, for which Ford had ample precedent in

Philaster, no neighbouring power to which the unhealthy
condition of Cyprus might lay it open to attack.

Our commonwealth is sick; 'tis more than time
That we should wake the head thereof ...

(II.1:p.24)

but after Sophronos has thus confided his fears to Aretus the
Prince's tutor, the action begins to concentrate not on the
sickness of the State but on the diagnosis of that of Palador.

In this semi-allegorical conception of the plot Ford is again
making use of something acceptable to the Caroline private
theatre audience with whom Jonson's *The Magnetic Lady* and
The Staple of News and Cartwright's masque-like Platonic
dramas — dissimilar plays but with the same formal tendency
— were generally in favour. The State of Cyprus is also the
state of man; Palador is its head, Rhetias the honest critic is its
conscience, Eroclea is its heart and inspiration, and to Corax
the physician

Men are like politic states or troubled seas,
Teased up and down with several storms and tempests.

A glance at the list of characters will show how closely knit are
their relationships. The Prince and his cousin Amethus are
half-betrothed to Eroclea and Cleophila, the daughters of
Meleander. Menaphon, destined to marry Thamasta, sister to
Amethus, is the son of Meleander's brother Sophronos. The
celebration of all these marriages makes of the Court of Cyprus
an interrelated and interdependent family group, while the
few remaining characters, even those in the comic sub-plot
surrounding the foolish courtier Cucculus, are closely
involved in the main plot as personal attendants and aides.
Ford is inclined to closely-knit groupings, but in no other of
his plays is there such deliberate linking of the characters, like
the limbs in a body, as here.

There is of course one notable exception — the physician
Corax, whose importance is in the life-giving influence which
he brings from without. In this small community Corax is an
increasingly dominant power when he sets to work within it,
but that he feels himself an outsider is stated with some
explicitness. While he meditates the masque he regrets, with

the outsider's bitterness, the restrictive obligations of a Court
appointment:

> To waste my time thus drone-like in the Court
> And lose so many hours as my studies
> Have hoarded up is to be like a man
> That creeps both on his hands and knees to climb
> A mountain top ...
> I need no prince's favour; princes need
> My art; then Corax be no more a gull;
> The best of 'em cannot fool thee.
>
> (III.2:p.44)

Corax is rather artist than physician and the artist is more
princely than the prince. His detachment creates a natural
affinity with Rhetias, and their partnership is sealed in an
interesting episode of 'flyting' between the pseudo malcontent
and the pseudo stage physician, clearly intended as a parody of
the early Jacobean 'characters' so much loved and used by
Webster. Rhetias accuses the physician (I.3:p.18f.) —
'Mountebanks, emperics, quack-salvers, wizards, alchemists,
cast-apothecaries, old wives and barbers, are all suppositors to
the right worshipful doctor' — the list is a fair cross-section of
the Jacobean underworld. He continues: 'Thou art in thy
religion an atheist, in thy condition a cur, in thy diet an
epicure, in thy lust a goat, in thy sleep a hog ... Physicians are
cobblers, rather the botchers, of men's bodies.' And Corax,
perversely identifying Rhetias with the conventional malcontent, gives as good as he gets: 'Thou affectest railing
only for thy health; thy miseries are so thick and so lasting,that
thou hast only one poor denier to spend on opening a vein ...
the best worth in thee is the corruption of thy mind, for that
only entitles thee to the dignity of a louse, a thing bred out of
the filth and superfluity of ill humours. Thou bitest anywhere
... thou art fortune's idiot, virtue's bankrupt, time's dunghill
manhood's scandal and thine own scourge.'
    All this recalls not only the shape and style of the 'characters'
and their use in drama, but also the traditional malcontent and
knavish physician of Jacobean tragedy.[3] Here however, the
'flyting' is clearly a joke — Rhetias laughs and Corax
dismisses it with 'these are but morrows between us'. The

intention is evidently both to please the audience with old favourites and to clear away traditional associations in the theatre so that this strange but logical partnership can get to work. As usual Ford selects for the traditional concept precisely what he needs; it is honesty, not the rancour of the malcontent in Rhetias, the art, not the predictable methods, of the Doctor that can heal this community. Brief as it is this lively passage, no doubt entertaining to a contemporary audience, has the effect of focusing upon the benign purpose of two otherwise stock characters. The function of Corax supported by Rhetias in this early part of the play is to draw both lesser and principal characters together in the first climax of the action, the visual climax of the masque in which the whole Court is assembled and attention directed upon the Prince.

The scantiness of material in the main plot surrounding the Prince is probably intentional. Ford's determination to strip the story of every non-essential necessitates keeping the Prince as far as possible out of the action until the second climax, when Eroclea returns in her own guise. Meantime the concern of the courtiers and occasional hints from Parthenophil's evident distress keep him in mind and at the same time preserve the sense of mystery which Ford associates with mental malaise. The effect of his rare, but emphatic appearances and abrupt departures is an impressiveness which makes the breakdown of his reticence the more dramatic. Corax's description of love melancholy evidently wakens Palador to an awareness of his own need. We have no soliloquy, no adventitious aids to interpretation of his state of mind, until the disappearance of Parthenophil after this episode draws from him an outburst which astonishes his Court —

> Ye have consented all to work upon
> The softness of my nature; but take heed:
> Though I can sleep in silence and look on
> The mockery ye make of my dull patience
> Yet ye shall know, the best of ye, that in me
> There is a masculine, a stirring spirit ...
>   'tis not your active wit or language
> Nor your grave politic wisdoms, lords, shall dare
> To checkmate or control my just demands.

                                                    (p.70)

His demands are as unjust as the King's in *Philaster* for the
immediate return of his lost daughter; the missing Parthenophil must be restored without gainsaying, for, as he
confesses to Rhetias in a calmer moment,

> he is like to something I remember
> A great while since, a long, long time ago.

(p,71)

As yet Palador is unable to discern or accept why Parthenophil
is of such importance to him since he still believes Eroclea
irrecoverably lost. 'Rare delusions' cheat him and nothing
connects. There is the 'strange masque' which 'puzzled' his
understanding and the boy haunts him; his 'very soul of reason
is troubled'.

Now this is a realistic impression of an introspective man in
a neurotic state of mind, closer to living experience than to
theory, and like the typical neurotic he is ready to suspect
'some practice, sleight or plot'. But when Rhetias leaves him
to bring in the supposed Parthenophil in woman's dress,
Palador, meditating like Hamlet on the perfection of man,
begins to understand his own disorder:

> The music
> Of man's fair composition best accords
> When 'tis in consort, not in single strains:
> My heart has been untuned these many months
> Wanting her presence in whose equal love
> True harmony consisted.

(p.72)

Only in the true love, for him of Eroclea, can Palador recover
in himself the harmony he has lost, the 'concord in discord' of
Parthenophil's music described earlier in the play, for it is a
harmony of two natures, not generated from one alone, and
only by reunion with Palador can Eroclea return to life.

Ford is of course drawing upon the popular neo-Platonic
idea of 'equal love' destined between two partners, but this is
only his starting-point. Eroclea, who has now entered behind
in her own dress, continues his thoughts; without this inner
harmony man's life is no more than 'the numbering of
minutes by the fall of sands'. This part of the episode has

something of the manner of the classical *commos*, a patterned
dialogue with a musical formality having little to do with
either character or action but falling like an interlude of verbal
music across a situation of dramatic tension. The device was
apparently acceptable in a theatre where music was in general
demand.[4] Ford used it again in *The Broken Heart*, his only
other play for Blackfriars, but — significantly — in none of the
five plays which he wrote in his maturity for the Phoenix.

Here the meditative quality of the lines combined with their
formality suggests the plight of deeply sympathetic natures
who cannot touch. Palador resists his own fulfilment, Eroclea
cannot grasp her happiness; the one is moved to anger, the
other falls back into morbid inertia, and for the next forty lines
the lovers strive and fail to communicate. Eroclea is so 'worn
away with fears and sorrows' that his

> life-quickening presence
> Hath scarce one beam of force to warm again
> That spring of cheerful comfort which youth once
> Apparelled in fresh looks.

But Palador cannot rid himself of his own persistent fear of
illusion. The more Parthenophil seems to identify with
Eroclea the more he feels betrayed.

> Cast thy shape off,
> Disrobe the mantle of a feigned sex
> And so I may be gentle; as thou art
> There's wichraft in thy language, in thy face,
> In thy demeanours: turn, turn from me prithee.
>
> (p.73)

The hesitations, the withdrawals, the slow dawning of truth,
recall Pericles' discovery of Marina, and like Pericles Palador
is overcome by joys that come too swiftly. 'Let me by degrees
collect my senses', he begs, and still he is afraid to yield — 'I
may abuse my trust.' But he has recovered sufficient poise to
question Eroclea objectively as Pericles questions Marina:

> Tell me thy country. — Cyprus. — Ha! Thy father? —
> Meleander. — Hast a name? — A name of misery;
> The unfortunate Eroclea. — There is danger
> In this seducing counterfeit.
>
> (p.74)

And after vain struggles to resist what Palador later calls 'that
eternal mercy which protects us', he ends with a simplicity in
which Ford is a master — 'Come home'.

This gamut of mood, of tone and pace in a brief episode
which begins with a Platonic idea expressed with classic
formality and ends with the directness of plain speaking and
thinking, is worth noting; but the total effect as compared
with the recognition scene in *Pericles* is musical rather than
dramatic. It is the type of episode which Beaumont and
Fletcher had made popular in the private theatre, but for Ford
its meditative manner enabled him to epitomise in a form his
audience could accept, not only a disturbed state of mind, but
the effect of that mental state upon the will and judgement.
When we see Palador again it is as a Prince, not only in fact,
but in renewed vigour and responsibility as the play moves
towards the reinstatement of Meleander — and with him the
restoration of well-being in Cyprus.

The scene changes to the castle in three episodes; the first
comes immediately after that in which we first hear of
Meleander's fate, (II.2) the second (IV.2) between Thamasta's
capitulation and the return of Eroclea to Palador, and the last
occupies the whole of Act V. The spacing of these episodes is
important to the theme, for Meleander's sufferings, so
carefully removed from the Court, and the wrongs which
caused them, are the hidden source of sickness in the state of
Cyprus. Meleander's castle has an emblematic significance, for
here despair and anger overbalance Cleophila's love and
patience and it is here alone that the root of past evils can be
destroyed by the rejuvenated Prince'. Here too all the characters
gather to regain their equilibrium and fulfil their destinies.

A reminder of King Lear's sufferings was evidently essential
to Ford's design. Meleander becomes a living symbol of the
consequences of man's injustice to man, and as such he must
dominate those who come to look on his misery. But the scope
of the play is limited. When Lear cries 'O you are men of
stones', no one on stage or in the audience goes unrebuked, but
the cosmic proportions of Lear's prophetic vision of human
evil, in the detachment of age and madness, are no part of
Ford's purpose. Corax, who takes charge of Meleander as soon
as   Paelador   is   reunited   with   Eroclea,   disposes   of
misconceptions for the benefit of Rhetias — and the audience:

Rhetias, 'tis not a madness but his sorrows —
Close-gripping grief and anguish of the soul —
That torture him; he carries hell on earth
Within his bosom.

(IV.2:p.63)

Meleander is a storm-centre of conflicting passions. Anguish
at the loss of Eroclea is exacerbated not only by dishonour —
his own and hers — but also by disillusionment with princes
and princes' creatures, a disillusionment better understood by
a contemporaty audience than by one of the present day.
When, accompanied by Menaphon and Parthenophil,
Amethus visits him, the old man greets him with a torrent of
scorn in which all the worldly evidence of greatness is reduced
to 'good cheer' for worms; after which with a venomous
personal thrust he presents Cleophila — 'You, you, the
Prince's cousin, how d'ye like her?' (II.2:p.39), and Amethus,
in shame at the bitterness he cannot alleviate, can make only a
broken reply — 'My intents Are just and honourable.' It is this
destructive urge to make a past wrong violate a present good
that draws from Parthenophil the comment — 'This sight is
full of horror.'

By assuming the role of a father similarly distressed in the
loss of a daughter Corax hopes to channel Meleander's
tempestuous thoughts so that his mind can detach itself from
the obsession of his own sorrows. Dramatically the effect is to
distance the situation so that when unwonted pity moves the
patient to prescribe for the doctor there is a noticeable
loosening of tension —

If thou canst wake with me, forget to eat,
Renounce the thought of greatness, tread on fate,
Sigh out a lamentable tale of things
Done long ago and ill done; and when sighs
Are wearied piece up what remains behind
With weeping eyes and hearts that bleed to death.
Thou shalt be a companion fit for me,
And we will sit together like true friends
And never be divided

(IV.2:p.67)

Meleander's grief is transmuted into verbal music which may owe something to Marston, [5] and in the momentary stillness which this passage seems to create it is in terms of music that he sees in Cleophila the 'well ordered' quality he lacks in himself:

> The model of the heavens, the earth, the waters,
> The harmony and sweet consent of times ...

> (p.68)

This concept of musical harmony between things different, first stated in Parthenophil's contest and recalled in the restoration of Eroclea to Palador, is functional here, where its recognition marks a first step in Meleander's rehabilitation.

When in the final episode he wakes like Lear from a long sleep to find himself clothed and barbered, the time is ripe for Palador to restore the justice that his father violated, so that

> 'twas a prince's tyranny
> Caused his distraction, and a prince's sweetness
> Must qualify that tempest of his mind.

> (IV.2:p.63)

Palador is the actor, but the episode is still dominated by the 'art' of Corax. Having set the patient's mind towards his own cure, Corax stages Palador's reinstatement of Meleander in his rightful honours, but the staff and patent of office represent not only the dignity he has lost and now recovered, but in addition the rewards of his sufferings. Palador is more than just, he is generous. This belief that the best way to restore a man's equilibrium is to endow him with honourable responsibility we shall meet again at the close of *The Broken Heart*. Here at each stage the Prince is the absent donor, yet Meleander remains singularly unmoved until Sophronos brings, again as a gift from the Prince, the miniature of Eroclea which the latter has worn in his own bosom. Then speech tears from him:

> what earthquakes
> Roll in my flesh. Here's prince and prince and prince,
> Prince upon prince ...
> Be thy enchantments deadly as the grave
> I'll look upon 'em.

> (V.1:p.85)

Meleander has reached a climax; he can both think of princes rationally and face the reality of his joy when Cleophila presents at last Palador's ultimate gift, the long-lost Eroclea who alone can liberate him from the effects of the wrongs he has suffered.

> Here let your cares take end; now set at liberty
> Your long-imprisoned heart.
>
> (p.86)

It is now Meleander's turn to struggle for continence, and in a startling image he confesses to a new kind of confusion:

> My tears like ruffling winds locked up in caves
> Do bustle for a vent; — on t'other side
> To fly out into mirth were not so comely.
>
> (p.87)

Some of the most moving moments in this part of the episode are pointed with a delicate humour. It is as if the main characters had plumbed that depth of experience where the tragic and the comic begin to enrich one another. The transition is not easy, but with a few deft touches Ford presents Meleander no longer as a monument of grief but as a human being. Joan Sargeaunt notes the 'subtle distinction' between Meleander's attitude to his daughters.[6] Cleophila he values deeply and has come to rely upon, but with Eroclea there is a closeness which, even in this brief space, is expressive in teasing and gentle scolding. When, like Cordelia, she finds language inadequate, he rallies her with 'Wherefore drop thy words in such a sloth As if thou wert afraid to mingle truth With thy misfortunes?', and his old-man's wonderment is more than half amused as she begins to tell her story — 'And still thou wert a boy?'

A dominant idea here and in the earlier recognition scene, and underlying the thought of the play, is that of home-coming. Palador welcomes Eroclea 'home' to himself, Cleophila bids her father 'welcome home the solace of your soul', and at the close of the play Rhetias tells how Sophronos watched over all their fortunes until by his care 'we were all called home'. It is in this spirit that the two princes claim their 'own' and Thamasta is given to Menaphon. In this triple marriage the characters recognise their kinship while even the minor characters are accorded a place and contentment. Cyprus has come home to itself — and that not by the operation of a political leader nor even directly of a prince, but by the care of a physician, the constant target of the Jacobean stage. In the purview of the play the physician's skill becomes an art — to control, to shape and set in order the passions of men, and so to achieve a concord in discord in a whole community. This novel treatment of a familiar stage figure proves its usefulness in the final act, where, however loosely, Corax links the romantic and clinical aspects of the play.

Now this carefully conceived and crowded episode of settlement and reconciliation is seen within the framework of the reconciliation scene in _King Lear_. It does not of course bear comparison. The scene in _King Lear_ owes a good deal of its effect to its brevity and concentration; here the all too obvious superficial similarities are a drag on the attention so that the restoration of Meleander through material honours, however impressive the pageantry of their presentation may be, comes as something of an anti-climax. When the reunion with Eroclea actually occurs the magic is gone. In fact the scene is over-weighted with psychological matter; Meleander is to find his soul's satisfaction in Eroclea but he must also recover his faith in princes. The similarity between the two aged victims of a corrupt world is evidently intended to highlight both the regeneration of Meleander, to which the whole action has been moving, and the healing qualities of Eroclea's love. But there is no real parallel between the bitterness of Meleander's derangement and the universal significance of Lear's mental disintegration, nor is Eroclea in any sense a Cordelia. Ford's task might have been easier if he had resisted the temptation to reproduce the reconciliation scene from _King Lear_.

Ford is often criticised for failing to make his comic characters either amusing or convincing. But Cucculus, the foolish courtier of the comic plot, has a use and a place throughout the play. His constant posing as a Platonic lover renouncing a lover's reward, especially in the episode in which he enumerates for the benefit of his page, the boy-disguised-as-girl Grilla, all the ladies in the Court whose love affairs take his fancy as ready conquests of his own, is a possible satire on neo-Platonic romanticism, and his exchanges with Grilla are often entertaining. The same cannot be said of Trollio, Meleander's attendant fool, perhaps suggested by Lear's fool, who has little dramatic function and whose clumsy attempts at humour encumber the action.

In this play, perhaps above all his other work, Ford asks of us a willing suspension of disbelief. As far as plot is concerned motivation is not of paramount importance — for instance there is an obvious query as to Rhetias' reasons for withholding from Palador the secret of Eroclea's return when the Prince confides to him his abiding love for her. While the play is in progress or in reading the matter seems irrelevant; at the same time the play cannot be altogether a dream world, since Corax carries out his clinical experiments within it. The weakness of the play, and one which we have to accept, is that the two disparate facets of the action do not entirely cohere.

Perhaps partly as a result of this dichotomy, Ford seems determined to shock the audience into attention from time to time by the use of imagery which rivals some of the worst excesses of metaphysical poetry. For instance, when Eroclea and Cleophila on meeting fall into one another's arms in tears, Palador intervenes with

> We must part
> The sudden meeting of these two rivulets
> With the island of our arms.
>
> (V.1:p.82)

On the other hand the play is rich in verse which depends for its beauty on verbal music. Few poets could use assonantal effects and simple repetition with greater sensitivity than in the often-quoted lines —

> something I remember
> A great while since, a long, long time ago.

or

> things
> Done long ago and ill done.

In both passages the meaning is carried by the heavy monosyllables so that the line lengthens like a sustained breath.

This kind of writing for the stage demands an intimate theatre where facial mobility and the movement of hand or limb can make a natural impression at close quarters. The feeling of intimacy throughout the play has been commented on and the simplicity of the staging is contributory. The number of stage localities is at a minimum — a hall or common meeting-place in the Prince's Court, the main chamber in the castle, serve for most acting areas. The discovery of the sleeping Meleander may have been managed by a simple withdrawing of the hangings[7] which as suggested in the previous chapter probably stretched across the entire stage, and the hangings may have been used again to facilitate the arrangement and discovery of scenic effects during the masque. The vantage-point from which Menaphon looks down upon Thamasta and Parthenophil is obviously one of the window spaces opening out of the Blackfriars stage front, not an upper stage. Although stage directions make no particular demand for music, the masque and the pageantry of the final scene are opportunities for musical accompaniment and the style of the whole play, as well as a good deal of its content, is musically conceived.

But Ford is doing a good deal more than merely conforming to his theatre. His general purpose in handling his sources seems to be a simplification — almost a debunking — both of romantic idealism and current ideas of mental disorder. Even Trollio has his uses with his prescription of 'warm porridge' for his deranged master! As with the malcontent and the stage doctor Ford's tendency here is to expose either fashionable idealism or traditional assumptions to the realism which would inform his following work. Under cover of pleasing the taste of his audience Ford seems to be feeling round it — cajoling a sophisticated public into liking what was good and lasting in both new and old dramatic material. Thus for Ford the theme of melancholy was not an end in itself but a starting-point for a new psychological attitude in drama. However it might look to an audience who came to the theatre for pure recreation, for the dramatist it was a new beginning. After Shakespeare Ford was, I believe, alone in exposing the romantic conception of the lost and the found to the tensions of tragedy. For while the 'cures' of Palador and Meleander are planned step by step through the professional skill of Corax, they are evidence of an ordeal within the personality which neither Corax himself nor any of his helpers can fully penetrate. To achieve all this and at the same time bend the traditional figures and themes to the intention of the play was a mastery.

Later Ford would experiment with subjects and patterns of drama which would demand what he could give best in dialogue and character response — the poetry of directness. For the time being the themes he had chosen gave him the opportunity to show in a poetic drama, often approaching the lyrical, that the nobility of man is attained not through a conflict between nature and nurture but by their partnership. Nevertheless the position in society of the individual whose vision is different would trouble and tease him. This is the problem he was to handle when he returned to the Phoenix Theatre with *'Tis Pity She's a Whore*.

3 The Revenge Motive in *'Tis Pity She's a Whore:* a play for the Phoenix Theatre

> I hold fate
> Clasped in my fist, and could command the course
> Of time's eternal motion, hadst thou been
> One thought more constant than an ebbing sea.

These lines in which Giovanni blames the frustration of his hopes upon his sister's infirmity of purpose, are a statement of one polarity of meaning in *'Tis Pity She's a Whore*; the other is implied in his final appearance brandishing on his dagger the heart which he has torn from her body. His defence of his incestuous love for Annabella, his resolute pursuit of action which he knows undermines the system of ethics on which the society of which he is a part is based, is undertaken not without anguished self-searching. He knows, and Anabella knows when she yields to him, that they bring upon themselves the combined forces of religion, family and society, compulsions before which they are guilty and which will ultimately destroy them. But they also know that for them their love is the only reality; ethically they admit that they are wrong, inwardly they know that they are fulfilling the destiny their natures have shaped for them — it is their 'fate'.

Nothing could better demonstrate Ford's belief in the future of his theatre than his persistent choice of the resistant or isolated individual in the four tragedies which probably followed *The Lover's Melancholy*. The realisation of such a character involved presenting an acute human experience in a personality stirred to its depths. In the Caroline theatre the material was new but it demanded a dramatic pattern which was old — the pattern of Revenge Tragedy. It demanded also a new awareness in the audience. In the three plays between *The Lover's Melancholy* and *Perkin Warbeck* there is a noticeable toughening of Ford's art, a poise and economy and a new kind of realism which he seems concerned to establish in the contemporary theatre. Yet Ford knew enough about audience

36

reaction to temper the impact of emotional shock. Similarities in *'Tis Pity* to *Romeo and Juliet* are well known. Giovanni's appeal to the Friar, Anabella's relations with her aged nurse, the embarrassing concern of her father to marry her well, and the disasters which follow the marriage were probably familiar enough to persuade a not very attentive audience that they were witnessing yet another story of star-crossed lovers. Meantime at every point of similarity the play enunciates its independence.

In contrast to Romeo's love-sick boyishness in the early part of Shakespeare's play, Giovanni is Ford's angry young man, but his anger is concerned less with values than with a basic principle of constancy to a conviction, a loyalty to the self which is rather outside the moral law than contradictory of it. From the opening of the play we know that he is doomed and his last appearance, when defeat and death are upon him, recalls the closing scenes of *The Revenger's Tragedy* and *Antonio's Revenge*. But his gesture is more than one of defiance; Giovanni's dagger with the heart impaled upon it is a symbol of violation.

There is no known source for this play although some critics believe it may have been inspired by the case of Sir Giles Allington, who was savagely punished in 1631 for marrying his half-sister's daughter.[1] Giovanni and Annabella are the children of Florio, a merchant of Parma, and the action of the play is set in the wealthy mercantile background of a typical city state. When Giovanni conceives his in-cestuous passion for Annabella he first asks counsel of the Friar Bonaventura, his tutor and the family confessor. He endures the Friar's reproaches and follows his advice to wrestle with himself in prayer and fasting, but when all this is of no avail he believes he is justified in revealing his love to his sister, who admits that she reciprocates it. The lovers consummate their union and for the moment are happy and fulfilled, but their dread is that Anabella may be forced into marriage. For while Florio is not a tyrannical father he expects his daughter to make a good match and hopes that she will choose between three suitors — Soranzo, a nobleman of Parma, Grimaldi, a Roman gentleman and nephew to the Cardinal, the papal nuncio, and Bergetto, a foolish but wealthy young heir. Having failed to move Giovanni, the

Friar now terrifies Anabella into submission with warnings of
damnation, counselling marriage as her only means to
salvation, and Anabella agrees to marry Soranzo. Under cover
of this marriage the lovers plan to continue their liaison but
when Soranzo discovers that Anabella is pregnant his faithful
servant, the Spaniard Vasques, worms the secret out of Putana,
Anabella's ageing nurse and confidante. Soranzo determines
to expose the lovers, and have his revenge, at a banquet to
which he invites the chief nobility of Parma. Solitary and
confined Anabella suffers another and, this time, a more
profound change of heart. Accusing herself of deadly sin she
sends a letter to Giovanni by the Friar to warn him of his
danger. But Giovanni, still unshaken, accepts Soranzo's
invitation and in an episode alone with his sister anticipates
his revenge by stabbing her to death himself. In the final
episode where he displays Anabella's heart before the shocked
assembled guests, Giovanni meets his death at the hands of
Soranzo's hired banditti, but not before he has given Soranzo
his death-wound. So, after all, Giovanni is the real avenger
and dies in triumph.

There was ample precedent for the use of the incest theme to
build up the action of Jacobean tragedy. Only a few years
previously Middleton had used it as the main interest in the
secondary plot of *Women Beware Women*; it is clearly stated in
Hamlet's opening soliloquy and Webster unmistakably hints
at it in the relationship between Ferdinand and his sister in
The Duchess of Malfi. But in all these plays the incest taboo is
designed to deepen the emotional effect of evil in the forces
which militate against the main character. On the other hand
in *A King and No King* Beaumont and Fletcher make the love
of a brother for his supposed sister the centre of the plot, but as
he has never seen her since childhood there is some excuse for
the attraction at their first meeting. In any case we are totally
reassured by discovering at the end of the play that the
supposed sister is of no kin at all. But as Benedict Nightingale
comments in his review of the National Theatre production of
this play 'Ford does not cheat'[2] — an observation which I hope
to show is true of Ford even in the highly problematic play
The Fancies Chaste and Noble. The uniqueness of *'Tis Pity* is
in the sheer audacity of Ford's handling of this difficult and
dangerous subject without a touch of prurience and with such

care to balancing the ethical standpoints surrounding it that critics are still divided as to the dramatist's intention![3] No one who allows the play to do its own work can fail to note the honesty and frankness with which the theme is stated and developed, or the lucidity of Giovanni's assessment of his position. The effect is to build up round the lovers an impression of inviolable innocence which, though perilously poised, is above the level either of the moral law or of the emotionalism inherent in a social taboo. The imagery connected with the lovers' relationship is designed to lift it above lasciviousness.[4] Embracing Anabella Giovanni asserts:

> Thus hung Jove on Leda's neck
> And sucked divine ambrosia from her lips.
>
> (II.1:p.115)

In turn, when challenged by Sorenzo Annabella speaks of Giovanni as a god:

> This noble creature was in every part
> So angel-like, so glorious that a woman
> Would have kneeled to him and begged for love.
>
> (IV.3:p.157)

Giovanni's lyricism on Annabella's beauty —

> View well her face and in that little round
> You may observe a world of variety —
>
> (II.5:p.129)

may briefly suggest Cleopatra, but this is an ideal of beauty to be worshipped rather than desired:

> For colour, lips; for sweet perfumes, her breath;
> For jewels, eyes; for threads of purest gold
> Hair; for delicious choice of flowers, cheeks;
> Wonder in every portion of that throne.

Annabella is a goddess, conferring life before pleasure, for if her eyes are stars they would 'like Promethean fire ... give life to senseless stones'. The one episode (II.1) in which we see the

lovers together and happy, may recall in its innocent dalliance
the love of Romeo and Juliet, but the impact of the scene is
rather ideological than passionate.

The early scenes of the play are designed to show Giovanni
less as a rebel than as a man in desperate quest of his own
proper way in life. The fate motive, recurrent in Ford's
tragedies, carries a new significance here as the mainspring of
the action.[5] To Giovanni fate is that which his nature dictates
for his self-fulfilment —

> 'tis not I know my lust
> But 'tis my fate that leads me on.
>
> (I.3:p.107)

He has despised his fate; he insists that he has 'reasoned
against the reason of my love' but when he yields to it
sufficiently to reveal his love to Annabella he is giving vent to
the demand of his whole being and of hers —

> 'tis my destiny
> That you must either love or I must die.
>
> (I.3:p.110)

In the context these lines clearly mean what they say — it is a
question of survival. This is the conviction that carries
Giovanni through the ensuing action until in the final scene,
although he knows his death is upon him, he can assert his
own triumph — 'For in my fists I bear the twists of life'
(V.6:p.179). Giovanni's constant insistence that he is moved by
his fate, understood in this sense, and not by lust is basic to the
firmness of purpose which is his role in the play; it is to this
that Annabella strives to be faithful in the early part of the
action.

Now this combination of an inherent innocence with
constancy is thrown into sharp relief by Ford's treatment of the
background in the sub-plots. Annabella's three suitors
illuminate three aspects of the society of Parma. Grimaldi is
the effete but ambitious aristocrat from Rome and we see him
first disputing precedence with Vasques, the trusted follower
of Soranzo of whom Grimaldi is bitterly jealous. Grimaldi
cannot lower himself to take 'no' for an answer as do Donado

and his nephew Bergetto when Annabella refuses the latter; rather he will stoop to murder though he knows it is an 'unnoble act'. When Grimaldi, intending to ambush Soranzo in the darkness of the streets, kills Bergetto instead, the ruthless candour of his confession to the Cardinal and the latter's cold perversion of justice on his nephew's behalf are presented as a denial of all that religion should stand for. Whatever we may think of Giovanni's conduct, that of the Cardinal and his protegé is a violation of established law and order in the interest of pride in high places. It is a first statement of a theme which runs through the play and which, significantly, is strongly projected in Soranzo, Florio's preference among Annabella's suitors.

Soranzo is carefully sketched as the direct opposite to Giovanni. We see him first reading Sannazar, well known as the poet of eroticism. His privacy is invaded by Hippolita, whom he has previously seduced and whom he has also abetted in persuading her husband Richardetto to undertake a dangerous voyage to Leghorn in the hope that he will not survive it. In fact Richardetto has returned and, disguised as a physician, awaits an opportunity to avenge himself, so that Sorenzo is both a tainted man and one marked for a just retribution. Virtually he is a murderer as well as a lecher; now it suits both his prudence and his inclination to make a good marriage with Annabella. His ruthless repudiation of Hippolita who now stands in his way, on the grounds that their liaison was in any case a wicked one, is a piece of priggish sophistry which deceives no one but himself.

Soranzo's story presents some sharp contrasts with Giovanni's own situation. Where Giovanni is actuated by deep conviction, Soranzo is led by mixed motives of worldly wisdom and desire; while Giovanni's faithfulness in love is unshakeable, Soranzo claims the right to change his mind. Twice in Vasques' unvarnished comments attention is drawn to Soranzo's total lack of compassion; his part with Hippolita is 'scurvily played' and his treatment of Annabella on discovering her condition appears 'inhuman and beastly'. In Soranzo love itself is violated. Hippolita's masque at Soranzo's wedding where, drinking by mistake of the poisoned cup which she had intended for him, she dies cursing the match, is a desecration of the marriage feast, but it is ironically recalled in Soranzo's other feast at the close of the play, where, again under Vasques' indifferent eyes, his own plan of vengeance is shattered by Giovanni's uncompromising gesture with the impaled heart. All this builds up the moral environment to which, with the most proper and kindly intentions and on the advice of the Friar, Florio has committed his daughter. We shall have a closer scrutiny of this wrenching of nature from its rightful course in *The Broken Heart*.

But the idea of violation has an even sharper edge in the handling of Bergetto in the comic sub-plot. It has been customary to dismiss the Bergetto scenes as extraneous relief. Ford was probably drawing upon the Ward in Middleton's *Women Beware Women*, but the difference is so acute as to suggest a serious purpose. The Ward was an embodiment of the grosser animal instincts, constantly associated with sensuality, choosing a wife on points as he would a stud horse. Bergetto is a childish simpleton, not far removed from the 'innocent' in the Elizabethan sense. His wealth exposes him to the greedy and unscrupulous but he himself is without vice and his idea of love is the comfort of a mother. His death scene is one of those rare, though not infrequent, instances in Ford of near transcription from life.[6] Bergetto's reaction to the ambush is shocked astonishment and his outcry that of a not very intelligent child: 'Oh help, help! here's a stitch fallen in my guts ... O my belly seethes like a porridge pot ... you may wring my shirt; feel here. Why Poggio!' (III.7:p.146), and finally with a natural shrinking from first experience of violence done to himself — 'Is this all mine own blood? nay then, goodnight with me' (p.147). The exclamation directed to his servant and companion — 'Why Poggio!' — is the protest of all innocents destroyed for no fault of their own through the devious practices and errors of cleverer and worse men. It is the death of a simpleton with its inevitable meaningless brutality, yet not without a touch of dignity, for Bergetto can remember in dying both his uncle and the 'wench' he had planned to marry, and he has a fitting epitaph in Donado's lines:

Alas, poor creature, he meant no man harm,
That I am sure of.

(III.9:p.148)

The death of Bergetto presents the violation of innocence in a corrupt society with something of the effect of senseless human disaster in a modern news film.

But it is in the Friar and in his relationship, primarily with Giovanni and secondarily with Annabella, that we reach the core of the play's intention. There is some emphasis upon the Friar's pride in Giovanni's distinction as a scholar as well as in his development as a worthy disciple. On his own part Giovanni trusts the Friar absolutely; he has 'unclasped' his 'burdened soul' to him, shown him all his thoughts, and in spite of the Friar's reproaches it is to him that Giovanni turns when it is feared that Annabella is pregnant. Yet unlike the gentle Friar of *Romeo and Juliet* this is a churchman first, with the conviction of traditional scholarship. The play opens unpropitiously with the churchman's clear distinction between the philsophy of the schools and the dictates of religion. Intellectual speculation may be right for the first but it is sinful for the second —

> better 'tis
> To bless the sun than reason why it shines.
>
> (I.1:p.99)

The Friar is making a travesty of reason. The issue was one on which heretics had burned and the point would not be lost on many in Ford's audience. Giovanni answers with a gentle appeal. Beauty is to him a divine directive to the good and therefore in reason, as opposed to 'customary form', there is nothing to forbid his union with his sister. Yet Giovanni is no irresponsible rebel; he knows his danger and feels the need of advice and an understanding listener. In both the Friar disappoints him — 'Is here the comfort I shall have?' Ironically it is in course of this dispute with one from whom he will hide nothing that Giovanni arrives at his settled conviction:

> It were more easy to stop the ocean
> From floats and ebbs than to dissuade my vows.
>
> (I.1:p.101)

The idea of the ebbing sea will remain with Giovanni to be applied to his sister with a different significance later.

Meantime it represents a state of indecision as abhorrent to himself as to his spiritual adviser.

When we see Giovanni again he is a trapped man; the Friar's prescribed self-examination has left him with two alternatives — the sin against religion which his love entails and the destruction of all 'harmony both in my rest and life'. His insistence that it is not his lust but the promptings of his own inmost being — his 'fate' — that leads him on is not a weak excuse for sin, as Professor Sensabaugh would have us believe;[7] it is a choice to which everything, good or bad, in his essential self impels him and when Annabella capitulates the simple ritual of the lovers' vows, recalling the unofficial marriage of the Duchess of Malfi with its equally grave implications, confirms the sense of that integrity which Giovanni's succeeding action is a persistent struggle to preserve.

When Giovanni tells the Friar of the consummation of his love the disaffinity between them reaches its climax. The Friar threatens Heaven's anger and the 'eternal slaughter' of the soul but against Giovanni's firm and patient reaffirmation of the Platonic arguments of the schools we sense his impotence. Annabella's beauty is an outward sign of inward virtue, therefore their love is virtuous 'since in like causes are effects alike' (II.5:p.128). To the Friar this is a perversion of knowledge; for the religious man nature's 'light' is no substitute for the teaching of the Church, but to 'Heaven's positions' nature is blind. Nothing could demonstrate more clearly the division between nature and nurture, in whose harmony lay the well-being of the main characters in *The Lover's Melancholy*. It is in this division, made vocal in the Friar, that the personality itself is violated in *'Tis Pity She's a Whore'*.

The first step in degradation comes immediately, when the Friar counsels Giovanni — 'Persuade thy sister to some marriage'. Giovanni reaffirms his position in the shocked reply — 'Why that's to damn her. That's to prove Her greedy of variety of lust.' Here is his answer to the Friar's warning of damnation and it is a turning-point in the play. For against the Friar's orthodoxy Giovanni sets his own distinction between a sin against an ethical code and a sin against the sanctity of love itself. It is now, when he sees Giovanni is immovable, that the Friar determines to undermine Annabella's resolution.

The Friar's so-called ineptitude and dubious moral position have become a commonplace of criticism. But the Friar is surely the strongest character in the play, the one to whom the main characters turn, on whom they rely for practical help as well as for advice, and, moreover, the one who makes the fullest use, according to his lights, of the opportunities his influence gives him. As the action develops the Friar becomes a figure of terror and it is thus that we see him dominating the cowering Annabella in the repentance scene.

In these melodramatic episodes it is often Ford's habit to leave a good deal of the interpretation to the actors, so that what looks like a loose link in motivation as we have it in the printed text may well be a deliberate *ad lib* invitation to the company. Here the bare stage directions, the behaviour of Annabella weeping and wringing her hands, 'kneeling and whispering' to the seated Friar, 'a table before them and wax lights' are all conducive to a dumb show in which the Friar becomes a projection of the fears of hell — a fitting introduction to his lurid description of the punishments of the damned which follows:

> There is a place —
> List, daughter — in a black and hollow vault
> Where day is never seen ...
>
> (III.6:p.144)

and the Friar brings home his exploitation of her childhood terrors with

> Then you will wish each kiss your brother gave
> Had been a dagger's point.

The words are prophetic, for she will find his dagger's point as he gives her his last kiss. But the Friar wastes no time in acting upon her submission to clinch the marriage contract with Soranzo. For better or worse the Friar is the most competent person in the play and it is his ruthless exploitation of the

emotions of the main characters and of the hold that traditional sanctions have upon them, that carries the action to its
climax in 'Soranzo's ill-omened marriage. The situation is the
more impressive dramatically in the undeniable logic of the
Friar's position. As compared with the Cardinal there is no
graft, no mixed motive in this priest; he acts upon the
conviction of his training that, by whatever means, souls must
be saved, a conviction that nevertheless hands over Annabella
and Soranzo to a union which can only degrade them both and
ultimately destroy them.[8]

Even so there are limits to the Friar's power to neutralise the
influence of Giovanni, as is clear enough in Annabella's
Cleopatra-like eulogy on her lover when, at bay, she faces
Soranzo on the discovery of her pregnancy — evidence, if any
were needed, that the continuance of their liaison is to be
understood. But when her defences finally break down and she
repents in earnest, true to type and warmed by apparent
success the Friar is there again to assist and applaud and, this
time, to present Giovanni with the evidence in Annabella's
letter of his own confusion in terms of crude fact. And now,
having totally misunderstood the nature of both his charges,
inflexible in his moral stance against the dangers of reason and
individualism, the Friar withdraws to leave the issues he has
set in motion to resolve themselves. Nothing could better
demonstrate the indifference of the Establishment in a time of
need than this retirement of a spiritual and intellectual
guide from the world of real consequences which he wishes
he had never entered. If the Friar is no corrupt churchman
neither is he an aged well-wisher. Ford has made of
Shakespeare's attractive but unfortunate spiritual comforter
a projection of a ruthless moral rectitude. The Friar is
conceived and deliberately presented as a destroyer of the
human spirit.

Hearing that their love is betrayed, that Annabella had had a
change of heart, Giovanni knows himself to be alone.
Character development in Giovanni is worth watching; as
Romeo puts on maturity at the news of Juliet's death, so
Giovanni puts off the gentleness and trustfulness which are
apparently germane to his nature to put on the cold anger of a
desperate man. At last he sees the traditions in which he has

been reared, the Friar's training, even the idealism of his love, for what they are worth. All that is left is loyalty to himself and the conviction that has carried him — that of two rights he has chosen the greater, that of two sins he has committed the lesser. It is in this spirit that he responds to Soranzo's invitation to the banquet — 'Tell him I dare come'.

The brief episode between the lovers is a succinct statement not only of the action that has led up to it but also of a basic divergence which redefined the play's intention. Annabella has not Giovanni's training in reasoning and argument to defend her against the Friar's 'brainwashing'. Her sole guidance is the breeding she has received as the daughter of an important family, destined to marry either wealth or rank; she is a child of nurture rather than of nature. She can reject Donado's proposal on Bergetto's behalf with firmness yet with courtesy and her consideration is combined with a forthrightness which wins his admiration. In the difficult scene of Soranzo's courtship when, watched by Giovanni, she parries his advances with wit and poise, it is with the sensitivity of a more experienced woman that, on seeing hurt feeling in her wooer, she changes her tone and, as with Donado, closes the conversation. The chink in Annabella's armour is her emotional reaction both to her religion and to her love. At heart Annabella is a traditionalist, and because she has less imagination than Giovanni, within her limits she is a realist. Thus while her deepest instincts prompt her to respond to Giovanni's love, she understands, with a clarity he will not permit himself, the facts of their predicament under the pressures of her previous training. It is this limited realism that comes to her aid in the final repentance scene. Whatever their love has been in the past Annabella now sees her part in it as lust. Her comment on beauty in this scene is a reversal of Giovanni's insistence earlier in the play that where beauty is virtue must needs be:

Beauty that clothes the outside of the face
Is cursed if it be not clothed with grace.

(V.1:p.165)

This implied criticism of neo-Platonic idealism marks

Annabella's break with her brother to face the logic of
damnation — unless time allows her to demonstrate her
penitence. The point is underlined by a clear echo of the scene
in which Marlowe's Faustus faces the abyss of hell. Here as
there, time is bidden to stand still and there is a verbal
borrowing when Annabella refers to the 'stars That luckless
reigned at my nativity'.[9] Like Faustus Annabella faces
imminent death and again like Faustus she has only one thing
left to pray for — time. That Annabella should be thinking
with the damned Faustus and that the Friar, whose imaginings
of hell have turned the course of the action, should pass under
her window at this point lends a terrifying credibility to her
own presentiment of 'The torment of an incontrolled flame'
(p.166).

It is this new Annabella who meets Giovanni in her
chamber. Time with its inexorable passing still haunts her
and there is a certain fitness in the baroque treatment of a
commonplace image on Annabella's lips:

> Know that now there's but a dining time
> Twixt us and our confusion.
>
> (V.5:p.173)

For Annabella's concern is to bring her brother back to the
crude realities of their situation; their death is upon them —
what will he *do*? — 'Some way think how to escape.' What is
now to Annabella an illusion of the inexperienced youth is
still to him the justification of their search for truth.

He opens the scene with a charge of inconstancy:

> What, changed so soon?...
> Or does the fit come on you to prove treacherous
> To your past vows and oaths?

Now the phrase 'does the fit come on you?' is an echo of
Putana's lascivious comment on their first union — 'and I say
still if a young wench feel the fit upon her, let her take

anybody, father or brother, all is one' (II.1:p.117). Giovanni's
words are a veiled accusation of lust. To this view of her
marital relations he opposes 'our simplicity', his final claim to
a love untainted by lust. To Giovanni Annabella's new
sophistication is another betrayal of faith: 'You'll now be
honest, that's resolved?' It is too easy to dismiss this line as a
sneer. Giovanni is making an ironic contrast between honesty
as the world knows it — the face-saving of the Cardinal,
of Grimaldi or Soranzo and finally and most important,
of the hollow pretence of Annabella's marriage to save her
'honour' — and the real honesty of their love which he has
tested by all the moral reasoning known to him. In his eyes
Annabella's wavering has led her to substitute the false for
the true:

> What danger's half so great as thy revolt?
> Thou art a faithless sister, else thou know'st
> Malice or any treachery beside
> Would stoop to my bent brows.
>
> (V.5:p.173)

Annabella has destroyed their defences against an alien world.
His insistence that but for her inconstancy 'I hold fate Clasped
in my fist and could command the course Of time's eternal
motion' is not as empty as it appears. Giovanni's words are
coloured both by Annabella's obsession with time and his own
clear vision of precisely where he and his sister stand and why
they have failed. Their true natures had been freed by their love
which seemed to survive even Annabella's marriage. Together
in the simplicity of their true union they could have scored a
triumph over the sophisticated world which the passage of
time could not alter — if she had been 'One thought more
steady than an ebbing sea'. This echo of his insistence to the
Friar that his vows could as easily be 'dissuaded' as the 'ocean's
floats and ebbs' has a touch of irony. Unimpeded nature has
been his guide but he has reckoned without Annabella's
character. No less than the Friar he has misjudged the mind he
tries to influence.

Professor Stavig believes that Giovanni is unsure of himself
in this episode, in that paradoxically urging his sister to pray

he is 'a sinner who desperately tries to justify what even he himself subconciously knows to be wrong'.[10] This seems to me an over-simplification of an extremely complex situation. Giovanni does not deny the existence of Heaven or Hell, he does deny the viability of a Heaven in which he and Annabella are divided. Like the Cardinal towards the close of *The Duchess of Malfi* Giovanni feels himself alone in an empty and hostile universe, and like the Cardinal considering the 'one material fire of hell'[11] he meditates on universals — that 'this globe of earth Shall be consumed to ashes in a minute'. Yet even this may be false — nothing is certain but their love. What we have here is a demonstration of the trammelling by traditional sanctions of a spirit badly bruised in its battle for freedom.

   Annabella's insistence upon the imminence of death evidently suggested to Ford the episode leading up to the death of the Duchess of Malfi. Verbal parallels are obtrusive:

> A dream, a dream! Else in this other world
> We should know one another.
> > *Annabella* So we shall.
> *Giovanni*
> Have you heard so?
> > *Annabella* For certain.[12]

(p.174)

As usual with Ford's borrowings the parallel points an interesting contrast. In distinction from the serene faith of Webster's Duchess and her companion, Giovanni's next question, in which the personal pronouns carry the emphasis, is vibrant with a simple dread of isolation —

> But d'ee think
> That *I* shall see *you* there? — *You* look on *me*?

(italics mine)

Giovanni's attempt to make a fair contrast between the 'laws of conscience and of civil use' which may 'justly blame us' and the true value of their love must, I think, be taken as a summary of the attitude to incest in this play:

> when they but know
> Our loves, that love will wipe away that rigour
> Which would in other incests be abhorred.
>
> (V.5:p.175)

Ford is at some pains to show that the play is about a true and
honest love, not about a perversion. A weakness in these
closing scenes is the obvious difficulty he finds in making the
point of view convincing, but it is one to which the evocation
of the Duchess of Malfi insensibly impels us.

In all this Giovanni is bracing himself to the deed to which
the whole action of the play, the purposes of other characters
in the main and sub-plots, the flaw in Annabella's constancy,
have been driving. All that remains to Giovanni is to save their
love from the last indignity — and again the time-factor is
important. He must anticipate Soranzo's vengeance, which is
to be the vindication of 'honour' as the Establishment
understands it, by killing her with his own hand, thus
justifying his own integrity and hers in the public
confrontation which is to follow. In answer to her question
'What means this?' he replies 'To save thy fame and kill thee
with a kiss'. The Friar's warning is realised and Giovanni's
kiss has become a 'dagger's point'.

The sexual significance of the dagger is of some importance
in the two last episodes. Here it lends a depth of meaning to
Annabella's last cry — 'Brother unkind, unkind.'
Bewilderment that love and cruelty should seem to identify,
anguish that her death should be at her brother's hand, and
above all sheer incredulity that she and her lover no longer
speak the same language, are summed up in this superb
understatement of the fundamental division between them.

The closing scene is closer to the masque than to an episode
in straight drama. It opens with the formal entry to the
banquet of the Cardinal and the States of Parma. Soranzo
looks round for Giovanni, who promptly appears
brandishing a heart upon his dagger — a heightened version
of the conventional figure of the avenger — boasting of what
he has done, 'proud in the spoil of love and vengeance'.

The violence of Giovanni's appearance and the deed of which he boasts have puzzled critics and must puzzle actors and producers still more. The impaled heart is comparable with the blazing star which appears at the close of *The Revenger's Tragedy* and if it is presented purely as a symbol the closing action seems to fall into place. The key to meaning is perhaps in Giovanni's lines —

> the glory of my deed
> Darkened the midday sun, made noon as night —
>
> (V.6:p.177)

which echo his previous claim that the deed he meditates will make the sun's splendour 'as sooty' as Styx. The ambiguity is surely intentional; from one viewpoint he has indeed darkened the noonday sun, from another he has outshone it. The concept is a figurative presentation of the duality which Giovanni has already recognised in their love as posterity will judge it.

The heart impaled on the dagger is both a sex symbol implying absolute possession and, more important, a gathering together in a strong visual impact of the sense of physical, moral and spiritual violation which has run through the entire action.[13] As a symbol it has been carefully prepared for in constant references to ripping or tearing apart of the breast, the heart, the soul.

In their first meeting in the play, when Giovanni declares his love, he bids Annabella

> Rip up my bosom, there thou shalt behold
> A heart on which is writ the truth I speak.
>
> (I.3:p.109)

When the Friar has listened in horror to Annabella's confession of incest he rebukes her in words which suggest the damage which is in fact being done to her — 'You have unripped a soul so foul and guilty ...' Soranzo, furious at Annabella's refusal to name her lover, declares: 'I'll rip up thy heart And find it there' (IV.3:p.158) — a foreshadowing of Giovanni's reference in the final scene to 'A heart, my lords, in which is mine entombed' (V.6:p.177). And all this culminates in Giovanni's insistence that 'These hands have from her

bosom ripped this heart' (V.6:p.178). It is a build-up of
suggestions which have their counterpart in the reiterated use
of the words 'confusion' and 'blood' and references
throughout to the heart, which Brian Morris notes in his
introduction to the play. As he there observes, *'Tis Pity She's a
Whore* is an 'obsessive play'.[14]

The immediate reaction to Giovanni's entrance is total
inactivity, as if time, which has at last capitulated to the lovers,
is now suspended altogether. What is being thrust before the
eyes of those he knows will judge him is a projection of that
'rape of life and beauty' which Giovanni's own hand has
denied to Soranzo but which the latter's mismarriage to
Annabella had begun. The pattern of the whole scene focuses
upon Giovanni's ultimate triumph in his claim to possession
of Annabella; finally it is Giovanni who breaks the spell by
stabbing Soranzo, thus bringing into action at last the faithful
Vasques who was evidently waiting for his master's cue.

In a sense the episode is a summary of the plot, for in it
almost all the characters are present and all take up the moral
or emotional attitudes which they have held throughout the
action. Florio dies in the breakdown of the family honour of
which he has taken care, cursing the son who has flouted it,
Soranzo in the now belated execution of the vengeance for
which he has intrigued, Giovanni in the wish that has
motivated him throughout — 'Freely to view my Annabella's
face'. Those that remain behave in character as we have come
to know them: the Cardinal, that opportunist churchman,
takes care to confiscate to the Pope's 'proper use' the worldly
goods of those who have died as a result of their own violence;
Richardetto, throwing off his disguise, declares himself the
stern supporter of law and order; while Vasques, triumphing
no less than Giovanni in illicit success, protests his fidelity as a
servant and his joy that a Spaniard can outdo an Italian in
vengeance. There is a touch of grim humour in his reply to
Giovanni's query as to who wounded him first — 'I was your
first man, sir.' It was thus that the Thames watermen claimed
their custom. Vasques has indeed become Giovanni's
ferryman in death and unwittingly fulfilled a need — a useful
servant to the last.

To the contemporary view such a story demanded a
scapegoat. It is difficult to realise nowadays how great a risk
the dramatist and the actors ran in putting such a play before

the public. Ford may not cheat but he knows how to be prudent. Characteristically he makes a virtue of necessity in the obvious choice of the unfortunate Putana. Building perhaps upon the looseness of Juliet's well-intentioned old Nurse, Ford creates in Putana the typical household servant, priveleged by age and often in the closest confidence with the family. Putana is expert in the crude facts of life. She can assess Annabella's suitors with fair discernment, as much in their sexual capabilities as in their material prospects. To her Sorenzo is the man for Annabella if only because he has proved his masculinity in pleasing the 'lusty widow' Hippolita. It is Putana who abruptly degrades Annabella's new-found joy — 'O guardian, what a paradise of joy Have I passed over' — with the savage disregard of moral sensibility that characterises her view of reality — 'Nay, what a paradise of joy have you passed under! Why, now I commend thee, charge . . . and I say still, if a young wench feel the fit upon her, let her take anybody, father or brother, all is one.' Again it is Putana's long experience that discerns the first signs of pregnancy in Annabella where the physician fails. Putana is not only of the earth, she is of the lower man, on a level where a moral code is irrelevant and behaviour a matter of horse-sense. As with Middleton's Widow in *Women Beware Women* age blunts her resistance to blandishments and her simplicity makes her an easy prey to the crafty Vasques. The plaints with which she confides to him Sorenzo's harsh treatment and the revelations which follow have a touch of authenticity — 'Doth he use thee so too, sometimes, Vasques? ... Do you think so? ... I know a little, Vasques ... Dost thou think so, Vasques? ... Thou wilt stand between me and harm?'

To dismiss the mutilation she suffers at his hands as mere sadism is too easy. Putana belongs to that level of human existence where such things can happen; the sentence of death by burning which the Cardinal pronounces is a hit-back by a society concerned to save face when its proper victims are beyond its grasp. In Putana Ford introduces a note of bitter comedy; it is with typical irony that the hitherto fair-minded Donado is made to comment on the fate prescribed for Putana, ''Tis most just', after which he receives his orders — 'Be't your charge, Donado, see it done.' And Donado — solemnly: 'I shall.'

Only a few years earlier Webster had used the Revenge pattern in his two great tragedies to examine the plight of the individual trapped in an effete society whose sophistications are wearing thin. Here Ford uses the same pattern to show a typical section of society rent to its roots, to expose the primitive and the fundamental in the human make-up and to set against them the dilemma of the innocent and the would-be honest in their search for integrity. No other dramatist had ventured to present the theme of incest with such frankness on the one hand and such restraint on the other. The play runs on a knife-edge between condemnation of the lovers and sympathy with the strength of their convictions. In Ford's handling this ethical dichotomy is not a theme to be resolved but a state of conscience to be reckoned with in the characters' struggle for poise. To try to read moral conclusions into the play is precisely what its whole bias warns us not to do.

Ford's principal innovation in this revival of the Revenge pattern was in transforming it into a struggle between two sorts of avenger. Soranzo is the representative of an outraged society, but he is himself, like the establishment he stands for, morally tainted. Giovanni, on the other hand, is the rebel and iconoclast, destroying the ethical basis of his own breeding as a citizen of Parma, yet borne forward and sustained by the conviction of his own integrity, so that finally the central character becomes both rebel and avenger. If, here and there, Ford was drawing on the *Duchess of Malfi* it is possible that Giovanni's equivocal position owes something to that of Bosola, but the difference is revealing. Bosola is both the agent and the avenger of his masters' crimes, but he has first, however reluctantly, subscribed to their position — he is of their world; whereas from the opening of the play it is clear that Giovanni's love for his sister has thrown into sharp relief the ideological gulf that separates him from his background. His tragedy is that nature and nurture are at grips in him.

There is a boldness about the conception of *'Tis Pity* that compels attention, but it is a play of extremes necessarily tending towards a violence with which Ford himself was perhaps not entirely at ease. The plot is overcrowded with matter and the characters so vividly delineated that it is only after several readings that the pattern resolves itself into a whole. That Ford was himself aware of this may be suggested in the abundance of cross-references, some of which have been noted above, of reiterated concepts and frequent symbolic action. The play appears to have been written and planned with meticulous care, and compared with earlier examples of Revenge Tragedy — in Webster and Tourneur for instance — it has a swiftness and coherence of style combined with a dextrous handling of disparate material unusual in Caroline drama.

In all three tragedies written for the Phoenix Ford seems to make full and often experimental use of the amenities and conventions of his theatre. In this play Hippolita's masque, and the banquets at Annabella's wedding and in the final scene, both probably brought in by tiremen, are opportunities for colour and pageantry calculated to please a Caroline audience, but each of the three episodes marks a climax of dramatic irony. Each begins with pleasurable expectation, each is a prelude to destruction. The use of the upper stage level, three times in this play, has some similarly ironic possibilities. From their vantage-point on the upper level, probably the gallery over the stage, Annabella and Putana comment detachedly and pruriently upon the suitors passing outside the house until Giovanni appears below, when Annabella abruptly — and significantly — decends to him (I.2). Meantime the scene changes by the simple means of Giovanni's leaving by one door to enter by another to what is now an interior. But the point has been made. The lovers are together, alone and vulnerable. Later, in the scene of Soranzo's wooing (III.2) stage directions specifically state that Giovanni enters the 'gallery' above and watches events from there. His exposure to the audience and concealment from Soranzo add considerably to the effect of a particularly tense episode. Annabella's letter was evidently thrown down from the same gallery, now described as a 'window' (V.1), perhaps reshaped by the arrangement of the hangings.

Scenes in semi-darkness, lit by candles or a 'dark-lantern', are used with considerable dramatic effect. The best example is Grimaldi's ambush in which Bergetto is killed (III.7), followed by the entrance of officers 'with lights' (probably torches) and two scenes later by the episode outside the Cardinal's gates. These may have been one of the double doors at the back of the stage, revealed by withdrawing the hangings during the previous short scene on the front stage. It is again in a night scene that Annabella is 'discovered' repenting before the Friar with a 'table, wax lights', etc. (III.6), and again the discovery was probably effected by the use of the hangings, for the scene opens out to include the main stage when other characters enter. Ford seems to have a fondness for discovery scenes but in his hands the 'discovery' was not a matter of practical convenience but rather a means of emphasising or giving point to the action; such scenes must be easily seen and heard. It seems to me that the bedchamber episode between Annabella and Giovanni (V.5) was not played on the upper stage but similarly revealed by withdrawing the hangings which would be closed at its ending ready for Soranzo's banquet to be brought on.

The unusual number of scene changes in this play suggests a very free use of the doors at the back and sides of the stage. Short scenes, probably acted well down stage, invariably precede or follow longer and more crowded scenes played upon the central stage and representing either the street or a room in either Florio's or Soranzo's house. It seems that the cross-hangings were in constant use and that properties were brought, arranged and removed behind them. In 'Tis Pity She's a Whore, probably his first mature independent play for the Phoenix, Ford was testing not only the reaction of his audience to a disturbing theme, but also the usefulness of almost every aspect of his theatre — and that with a careful and professional eye.

That the play should have been staged and filmed within the same year, 1972-3, raises some interesting questions. Spectacle and the excitement of its subject would make a predictable impact in its own period, but what is its appeal in ours? — its violence? its honesty? its individualism? — or a certain half-pleasurable uneasiness without which no sensitive reader or playgoer can leave the play? Whatever the answer, the survival value to posterity of 'Tis Pity She's a Whore lies in the profound human experience it conveys and in the relevance of the issues it raises to the problems of living.

4 Reassessment of the *Othello* Theme at the Phoenix in *Love's Sacrifice*

Of Ford's tragedies *Love's Sacrifice* is the most typically Caroline. The title itself was calculated to please; the idea of love sacrificed for honour, loyalty or friendship was a late Jacobean vintage which had not lost its savour in the Caroline theatre, and the inevitably associated theme of sexual jealousy, with its potential psychological implications and scope for intrigue, had been developed in the contemporary theatre by Massinger, Brome and Shirley. Superficially the audience at the Phoenix were being offered what they had come to expect, nor would the pattern or business of the play disappoint them. The convolutions of an intricate plot gather round several centres of intrigue all bearing upon the focal love triangle between the Duke, his Duchess and his friend. In the action the links are loose but the secondary plots are so clearly inter-involved around the Ducal Court as to create the illusion of a unity of place. This, combined with a cross-section of character types from the Duke, his family and principal courtiers to the parasite, the buffoon and the supposed idiot, maintains an unflagging dramatic interest. There is no lack of opportunity for colour, pageantry and display: for instance, the reception of the Abbot, the Duchess' funeral, both played on the entire stage with torches and candlelight, ask for lavish costumes and stage properties. On the other hand the masque in which Ferentes is killed is not only an episode of extreme tension based upon a familiar stage trick, it is also a sharp ironic comment on a phase of the action which began as light comedy. As we shall see later, there is some dramatic irony in Ford's use of the upper stage level; in fact the play is an interesting example of the experimental use of theatrical conventions and normal stage amenities in the contemporary private theatre.

Despite a good deal of not entirely undeserved criticism *Love's Sacrifice* repays many readings, for it constantly surprises us with something new and arresting. Matter from

'Tis Pity and also from *The Lover's Melancholy* is recalled especially in the sub-plots, but links with *'Tis Pity* are particularly strong and the more significant in that they recall what was probably most memorable in the theatre. Giovanni's dagger reappears in the bloody dagger which the Duke displays after killing Bianca, but more important perhaps is the preoccupation with the idea of digging in or stripping down the flesh to find the heart (or the truth), or to extract either heart or womb from entombment in the body.[1] This particular kind of violence colours *Love's Sacrifice* and *'Tis Pity*. Neither play can be precisely dated but these figurative affinities suggest that *Love's Sacrifice* was written soon after *'Tis Pity* and, since *The Broken Heart* bears fewer traces of Ford's preoccupation at this time with physical violation, probably between *'Tis Pity* and that play.

The overall purpose of *Love's Sacrifice* becomes the clearer by comparison with two other tragedies bearing on the theme of love, honour and jealousy on which it appears to be dependent. The sources of the story, if any, are unknown; but an obvious borrowing is from *Othello*, which the play in certain scenes repeats verbally as well as circumstantially, and another link is with Massinger's *The Duke of Milan*, published in 1623, which it strongly resembles in the pattern of the plot.

The main plot of *Love's Sacrifice* centres upon Philippo, Duke of Pavia, who has married a young wife Bianca, dowerless and of inferior birth, but of great beauty and graced with sweetness of character. His dotage upon her earns Bianca the enmity of Fiormunda, the Duke's widowed sister. The Duke has a trusted and presumably younger friend Fernando, whom he wishes his bride to know and value; and the inevitable happens. Fernando falls in love with Bianca, who after first rejecting his advances is driven by passion to confess that she returns his love but will kill herself if he seduces her, whereupon the lovers agree upon a platonic relationship. Meantime Fiormunda has conceived a desire for Fernando and sends D'Avolos, the Duke's Secretary and her own creature, to sound him. When she finds Fernando resistant she determines to ruin him. By observing his reactions on seeing a new portrait of the Duchess D'Avolos guesses his secret and thenceforward closely watches the lovers' every movement. Like Iago playing upon Othello, D'Avolos drops into the Duke's mind doubts of his wife's loyalty; like Othello, the Duke demands the truth and is brought to see Fernando and Bianca together in a scene slightly recalling the eavesdropping in *Othello*; and like Iago, D'Avolos spurs his master on to vengeance. But it is Fiormunda who nags him into heroic fury and it is she who stands behind him as he stabs his Duchess to death, only to find too late that the lovers were innocent of adultery.

But here is no Isle of Cyprus to isolate the lovers. Bianca, Fernando and the Duke are seen against a background, oppressively crowded and confined, of a Ducal Court which is obviously corrupt. Fiormunda has an eligible suitor in Roseilli, a kinsman of Fernando, whom for undefined reasons she rejects and, again with the help of D'Avolos, tries to keep out of favour with the Duke and away from Court. The Duke himself has a partiality for the Court Don Juan, the licentious but amusing Ferentes, who has got three women with child under promise of marriage and who meets death at their hands in the course of a masque. This sub-plot is not without its comic side and there is also the light relief of Mauruccio, an old courtier who fancies himself young and witty enough to make a conquest of Fiormunda. Here is a court to play the fool in as well as the traitor, and Roseilli proceeds to do the first in earnest by disguising himself as a 'natural' fool in order to insinuate himself into Fiormunda's private apartments as a gift from Mauruccio. So we have a network of spying and counter-spying, and the quality of one love is set off by the folly or fallibility of another.

In D'Avolos, his diabolic nature thinly disguised in his name *(diabolos)*, Iago has become the devil that Othello terms him,[2] and as Othello unsuspectingly relies upon Iago so the Duke unthinkingly depends upon D'Avolos. In both tragedies the tempter plays upon the husband's insecurity before his bride; both are older, both love blindly, and both are conscious of being at risk in their marriage choice, for Othello is a Moor and the Duke knows he has broken with family tradition in marrying beneath his station. There is also some correspondence between Desdemona's vulnerable innocence and Bianca's artless simplicity. But the differences are so marked as to imply a deliberate reassessment of *Othello*. To

Ford, as to some modern critics, the whole conception of the Othello-Desdemona-Cassio relationship is over-simplified. Suppose Cassio did indeed love Desdemona to the point at which concealment was no longer possible, how might it affect her relations with an older, imperious and very busy husband? And suppose Cassio's courtesan were of noble birth, born to command and experienced in intrigue? In Ford's assessment the question of Desdemona's loyalty might appear unnaturally isolated and therefore unconvincing.

Ford has modified the monumental starkness of *Othello* first by developing Iago's domestic machinations into a web of Court intrigue, secondly by exploring the complexities of the human character through the eternal conflict between love and loyalty and the desperate consequences of jealousy and hurt pride. That he has blunted the *Othello* theme should not blind us to what he has brought to it — the psychological analysis of a nature divided against itself in Bianca, and the carefully drawn fallibility of the Duke set against a complex of human relationships in which main and sub-plots are inter-involved.

Before going into further detail it is worth while considering the plot of *The Duke of Milan*, to which Ford may have been indebted. Sforza, Duke of Milan, has recently married Marcelia, on whose beauty and reciprocal love he dotes extravagantly. Unfortunately Marcelia's arrogant rectitude in the Duke's absence arouses the enmity of Mariana the Duke's sister and Isabella his mother. Sforza has given Mariana in marriage to his trusted and beloved friend Francisco. But Francisco is in fact a traitor, bent on repaying the Duke for his seduction and subsequent desertion of his (Francisco's) sister. When Sforza leaves Milan to treat with the victorious Emperor with whom he has been at war, he leaves Marcelia and the State to Francisco's protection, but so jealous is his love that he leaves with him a warrant for Marcelia's death should he not return alive.

Francisco now proceeds to undermine Marcelia's faith in her husband by showing her the warrant for her death but not the conditions under which it is to be carried out. He then makes advances to her which she rejects with regal indignation. His next step is to threaten to kill himself for love of her, confessing at the same time his suppression of the rest of

the Duke's commission. Unlike Bianca, Marcelia still shows
no sign of amorous response, but she is moved by his penitence
to grant his dangerous request to show him favour in the
Duke's presence. When the Duke returns successful, having
preserved both his own and his country's honour, he is
shocked at Marcelia's cool reception of him; whereupon
Francisco alleges that Marcelia is in love with himself and has
tried to seduce him. Determined to teach her husband a lesson
Marcelia meets him in defiance and abetted by Mariana and
Isabella, the Duke stabs her only to hear with her last breath
the proof of her innocence. Francisco's vengeance reaches
perfection when, disguised as a doctor come to restore her, he
paints Marcelia's corpse with lifelike colours containing a
deadly poison and Sforza dies in kissing her.

  Parallels with Ford's play are easily recognised — the doting
husband, the trusted but disloyal friend, the envious
kinswomen, the threat of suicide albeit in the opposite
character. But Ford's deviations from the pattern are still more
interesting. First the character of Francisco is split in two —
the trusted and basically virtuous friend (Fernando) and the
sinister intriguer (D'Avolos). Massinger's somewhat sketchy
envious princesses are merged into the formidible sister
Fiormunda, who not only exhorts the Duke to vengeance but is
also accessory to Bianca's death. State affairs, which occupy
some fine scenes in Massinger's play, have no place in *Love's
Sacrifice* where the emphasis is upon the dangers and follies
which beset the lovers, and whereas Massinger's characters are
types rather than people, who never move from the course of
action on which they embark, their counterparts in Ford's play
have the supreme human quality of unaccountability. While
Ford has deliberately complicated the *Othello* theme, he
has stripped that of *The Duke of Milan* to its essentials.
Comparison with either play suggests a desire to pursue
human motive and action to their sources in the individual
personality, but in the process he seems to impose upon the
Othello theme the pattern of a play based upon intrigue and
circumstantial surprises. However we assess Ford's debt to
either tragedy, this dichotomy at the root of his own play is
something that any analysis of its intention and quality must
reckon with.[3]

  The play begins with something like the impact of the

opening lines of Webster's *The White Devil*. 'Depart from
Court? — Such was the Duke's command ... Why then 'tis like
I'm banished!'[4] Like Webster's Lodovico, Roseilli is indignant
at what he feels to be an undeserved disgrace — that now peace
has been restored to the State he should be 'wiped off like to a
useless moth'. In a flash of insight Roseilli discovers for
himself and exposes to the audience the unscrupulous courtier
in D'Avolos and the malevolent but influential woman in
Fiormunda. But after this introduction we are shown an
intimate group of courtiers, all friends and, as is characteristic
of Ford's Princes' Courts, largely interrelated. Fernando is
Petruchio's nephew and a kinsman of Roseilli, and a family
atmosphere is created round Petruchio's anxieties over the
relationship between his daughter Colonna and the
irresponsible Ferentes, and by Fernando's undertaking to
school his young cousin. The total impression is of a Court
that has been harmonious and is now showing signs of a
breakdown which may isolate the few just men remaining — a
fitting prelude to the entrance of the Duke, Bianca and
Fiormunda.

In his opening speech the Duke displays the imbalance that
will destroy him: self-indulgent doting on Bianca's beauty,
self-applauding satisfaction in the possession of such a bride
in her and so trusty a friend in Fernando. He is a 'monarch of
felicity' and Fernando is 'a partner in my Dukedom .. we are
all one.' The extravagance of his assumptions and the danger
his marriage may stand in are suggested by the background
gibes of Fiormunda with Ferentes and D'Avolos and not least
by the taunt which she flings at Bianca's inferior birth and her
motive for loyalty to a Prince that 'thus advanced her'.
Bianca's cool reply is not entirely reassuring —

> Sister, I should too much bewray my weakness
> To give a resolution on a passion
> I never felt nor feared —
>
> (I.1:p.293)

for it suggests a dignity and simplicity of character vulnerable
and isolated in such an environment as this. The impression of
coming danger is strengthened by the pressing of Fiormunda's
suit through D'Avolos upon Fernando; the latter's skilful

parrying of his advances has some parallel with Bianca's
handling of Fiormunda's malice before the Court. In a single
scene Ford gets the whole plot under way with considerable
impetus and meanwhile quickens expectation of
developments to come.

The overall picture is defined in the following scene, the last
in the first act. The scene opens with the triangular comedy of
Ferentes' commitments in amours; the thrice-repeated pledge,
the three-fold reiteration of the promise — each time to a
different mistress — to be true 'only to thee, only to thee', is
entertaining enough to leave the moral issue at least
equivocal. But the comedy of debauchery is followed by a hint
of the tragedy which may result from lust in high places when
the characters interchange; Fernando replaces Ferentes, and
Fiormunda entering has her chance to woo Fernando face to
face.

Dismissing his attempt to warn her against desire by
praising her constant widowhood, she brings him to the point
by offering him her wedding ring, which she had promised to
bestow on no one but a second husband. The gesture is the
more sinister in that it recalls and contrasts with the Duchess'
delicate wooing of Antonio in *The Duchess of Malfi*. 'You
have made me stark blind' is Antonio's reaction, but Fernando
is all too clear-sighted. His comprehension of Fiormunda's
motives and the nature of the woman he has to deal with is too
great for his safety. The episode, brief as it is, in the context of
Ferentes' entanglements and with the deliberate echo of the
union of the Duchess of Malfi with her lover, suggests a
degrading of love to which Fernando's feeble excuse that he
has made a vow of celibacy is contributory. It is cut short by
Bianca's entrance to enlist Fernando's help in moving the
Duke to reinstate Roseilli. Her action — the first unselfish
action in the play — throws the other characters into relief: the
agitation behind D'Avolos' officious warning that the Duke
will be angered by interference with Roseilli's banishment,
Fiormunda's ill-concealed determination upon revenge — 'I'll
quit this wrong' — the Duke's intimacy, upon entering, with
Ferentes, whose debauchery we have just witnessed, his
irascible rebuke to D'Avolos, with its touch of childish
truculence, for misunderstanding his instructions. Against all
this is the serene confidence of Bianca, as yet secure in her

husband's love, thinking no more ill than Desdemona when she pleads for Cassio with Othello — 'I will adventure chiding' — and lastly Fernando's instinctive response to sheer innocence when he sees it:

> O had I India's gold I'd give it all
> T'exchange one private word, one minute's breath,
> With this heart-wounding beauty.
>
> (I.2:p.303)

It is some evidence of Ford's artistic economy that even the final lines of the scene are used to direct attention to something which will deeply affect the action later — the Duke's attachment to his sister. When Fiormunda's nose bleeds he is concerned even in his anger — 'Look to her ... but look well to our sister' — a trivial incident but, in Fiormunda's words, ''tis an ominous sign'. This scene in which nothing happens but in which everything of importance is revealed, with its constant movement, its variety of tone, feeling and pace is a rare piece of dramatic skill.

The development section, Acts II and III, is a careful exercise in dramatic acceleration. Act II is constructed largely round significant objects either real or imagined. In course of practising romantic addresses to his lady Fiormunda in the first scene, Mauruccio describes in detail his ideal gift to her, a dressing mirror in the form of a crystal heart hidden under a detachable leaf in the breast of a portrait of himself. To an audience who had recently witnessed in the same theatre Giovanni's display of the heart he has torn from his sister's body, this would have the effect of parody — the more so in that Mauruccio regards it, as Giovanni regards his act of violence, as a masterpiece of imagination.[5] Next come the actual portraits of Fiormunda and the Duchess which D'Avolos shows to Fernando in order to discover whether Bianca is indeed the object of his love. Fernando's preoccupation with that of the Duchess, his repetition of 'hair', 'lip', 'heart', point unmistakably to the folly of Mauruccio, but the idea of the afflicted heart persists. Fernando wooing Bianca speaks of his 'bleeding heart' and of himself as 'the coffin of my heart' which if torn apart will discover 'Bianca's name carved out in bloody lines' — a concept

which Bianca applies to herself at the close of the scene in
Fernando's bedchamber. Again, while there is an association
with the violence of *'Tis Pity*, the immediate link is irresistibly
with Mauruccio's portrait mirror and the burlesque of all the
courtship in the play in his fantasy passion for Fiormunda.
Significantly the first breakdown in Bianca's defences is
introduced by a game of chess in which Bianca loses her queen
'and nothing for it but a pawn? Why then the game's lost too.'[6]
The pawn has already been identified with Fernando in
D'Avolos' ironic comment as he watches the lovers unseen —
''tis a rook to a queen she heaves a pawn up into a knight's
place' (II.3:p.320). The total effect is to reduce the idea of love
to the level of semblance, or of the game. An undefined fate
may be approaching but the characters are — ominously —
still at play.

Act III is built towards a climax on a series of ironic
contrasts and significant happenings. Again the act opens
with comedy in the slightly formalised pattern of Ferentes'
entanglements. Two irate fathers, Petruchio and Nebrassa,
enter, each dragging a pregnant daughter; upon them comes
Ferentes, himself pursued by Morona in the same
predicament. It is a neatly shaped situation whose
embarrassments Ferentes cheerfully shakes off. But following
upon the scene of Bianca's confession at Fernando's bedside
the episode has an ironic overtone which we hear again in
D'Avolos' muttered comments on Bianca's unguarded
behaviour with Fernando in the following scene — 'Beshrew
my heart but that's not so good ... A shrewd ominous token; I
like not that neither' — interjections followed by another
significant reference to a game at maw in which 'Your knave
will heave the queen out or your king'(III.2:p.335-6). A similar
significance attaches to the entrance of Mauruccio with
Roseilli disguised as a fool, whom he presents to the Duke; the
point is made in the consequent talk of folly in the wise which
Bianca summarises with, to her, an unintentional irony which
D'Avolos immediately recognises as applicable to his own
purpose:

> True my lord, there's many
> Who think themselves most wise that are most fools.

(III.2:p.337)

But when the Duke's challenge to D'Avolos and his hints is followed sharply by Ferentes' murder during a masque, the action seems to stop short with disturbing suddenness. This piece of savagery in which the three women stab their victim, exulting in blow after blow, turns the humour of Ferentes' amours inside out. As so often with Ford the fate of an irresponsible or lightweight character becomes a significant business. Ferentes is the first character in the play to come to himself — 'My forfeit was in my blood; and my life hath answered it' (III.4:p.343) an implied warning that dalliance is over and other characters than himself will have to face reality. Considering the familiar criticism of Ford's management of comic sub-plots it is worth noting the care with which episodes in the Ferentes and Mauruccio stories are placed and the effect of this placing on the emotional slant of the play. But equally skilful is the dropping of both sub-plots at this crisis in the action — for with the masque which winds up the Ferentes plot Mauruccio's activities are also virtually over since he is himself partially implicated, and we see him again only at his dismissal with the ageing Morona as his bride. With the artist's economy, now that the lesser material has done its work, Ford clears the stage of all but the main plot for the final confrontations.

So close are the parallels with *Othello* in the middle scenes of the action that it is tempting to imagine that Ford wrote with a copy of the play at his side. But as usual with Ford's borrowings, the closer the verbal or circumstantial parallel the greater the contrast in meaning and attitude; so that for an audience familiar with its source the borrowed material serves to illumine the characters and their behaviour. We have already seen evidence of the Duke's febrile management of his Court; imperiousness rather than authority, truculence rather than just anger, impulse rather than judgement, condition his relations with other people. But his most dangerous weakness emerges at his first appearance in his unthinking acceptance of those he loves or finds useful. The favours he shows to Ferentes, whose open licentiousness he evidently ignores, is as much in character as his reliance upon D'Avolos, his undiscerning regard for his sister and even his deeper affection for Fernando and his devotion to Bianca. The great man cannot live without a prop; like Othello he can therefore be played

upon but for quite different reasons. Othello is ignorant of
sophistication, not of life, nor of humanity, and he succumbs
to Iago's temptation largely because his vision of life, though
egocentric, is too big for the world he lives in. But the Duke
knows neither the pressures of loyalty nor the nature of human
love; beyond the narrow circle within which he can wield un-
questioned authority he has learnt nothing and he understands nothing. As in *Othello* jealousy is rather in the tempter,
the unscrupulous contriver, than in the central figure; but
whereas we see Othello as the victim of a natural nobility of
heart, we witness the Duke, by his own weakness, encouraging
in Fiormunda a will to power which lets loose the destructive
force he failed to discern in D'Avolos. A climax is reached
when Fiormunda, left alone with Fernando (IV.2), suggests, as
Emilia suggests of Othello, that the Duke is jealous but when
under cover of a kindly warning she again, and more openly,
presses her suit and Fernando again, and more firmly by his
silence, rejects her, Fiormunda finally resolves upon a jealous
revenge — 'Change passion to contempt', she cries, 'Fool, he
shall learn I was not born to kneel' (IV.1:p.353).

After the shock of Ferentes' murder Fiormunda and
D'Avolos make a frontal attack upon the now frenzied Duke.
As Othello exclaims that he is on the rack, so the Duke begs
them 'Be gentle in your tortures' (IV.1:p.346). Like Othello the
Duke demands proof and like Iago, but with a nagging
brutality which Iago would never venture upon with his
general, D'Avolos presses home the shameful aspects of
marital infidelity, prodding his master's imagination until he
rouses himself to threaten the action his hearers hope and
expect of him:

> *Fiormunda.* Why now I hear you speak in majesty.
> *D'Avolos* And it becomes my lord most princely.
>
> (IV.1:p.347)

There follows a dramatic shock of which at this date few other
dramatists were capable. The Duke cuts across the dialogue
with a simple phrase — 'Does it?' The text suggests a sharp
pause, after which another quiet phrase — 'Come hither, sister
...' This is Ford's introduction, typically his own, to the
warning, again based upon Othello's colloquy with Iago, of

the consequences of trickery or, in this case, of female jealousy. It is one of those flashes of insight with which Ford likes to endow his weaker characters at moments of crisis. In his heart the Duke knows that something is wrong in his advisers; the sudden quiet utterance is that of his better self, the self that chose Bianca for better reasons than her beauty and Fernando for deeper uses of friendship than the comfort of a stronger nature than his own.

But the moment of perception passes and, again like Othello, the Duke, supported by his two tempters, kneels to make a formal vow of vengeance. The difference is illuminating. Othello calls upon the current of the Pontic sea and the marble heaven, Iago upon the elements, to witness to their pledge; the Duke can think only of ingenious plots and his own sacrifice of well-being and status should his purpose weaken. In *Othello* we are among titans, here we are in a confined world of little men. Henceforward the Duke's problem is not merely how to steel himself to his task but also how to identify what he sees in action around him, to distinguish between the false and the true.

This is his difficulty in the episode (IV.2) in which he warns Bianca of the danger threatening her — and incidentally makes a last appeal — by describing a dream in which he sees her trampling on his cap of state while he holds her 'hemm'd' in his arms. The passage recalls that in which Othello both weeps over Desdemona and accuses her (*Othello*, IV.2). But while Othello finds stability by raising his act to the level of an ideal sacrifice, however illusory, the Duke falters to the end, between blind rage and the wishful thought that he may after all be mistaken:

> I dream and dream anew ...
> these divisions so distract
> My senses that I take things possible
> As if they were.

(IV.2:p.355)

When later, after discovering the lovers in amorous conversation, he has Bianca at his mercy, sheer confusion as to what he sees before him racks him in nerve and judgement. She is the 'black angel', the 'fair devil' — even so perhaps she is capable of redemption. It is not humanity but inability to face up to an equivocal situation that makes him drop his weapon. Only Fiormunda's one-track mind can clarify the issue for him and hold him to his purpose. From his first entrance the Duke's ineptitude is exposed with a searching realism unusual in the Caroline theatre.

Again, while Desdemona's innocence is never in doubt, the problem of Bianca is complex. Her gentleness and modesty in face of Fiormunda's malice at the beginning of the play, her readiness to use her influence to aid those less fortunate than herself, combined with her staunch integrity when Fernando first tries to woo her, build up an ideal of feminine grace and dignity which we meet again in Ford's domestic drama. Bianca's is no cloistered virtue — she will 'adventure chiding' in a good cause. Her daring behaviour when after castigating Fernando's persistence she presents herself at his bedside, entirely at his mercy, is somehow acceptable. So also is the high idealism which prompts her to determine upon suicide should he take advantage of her confession that she loves him. Gratitude and affection towards an indulgent husband on her part and to an over-trusting friend on his, induce them both to face their dilemma squarely; and the Platonic love they agree upon is 'love's sacrifice' to preserve both love and honour.

But this typically Caroline conception, well-worn in the private theatre, dissolves in Ford's hands into a fallacy. In crude daylight the night's good intentions throw up an essential difference between the natures of the two lovers. Fernando's dearly-bought self-knowledge is a foil to Bianca's untrained innocence. For Bianca to resolve to do well is to do well; having put evil behind her she can enjoy the peace of a quiet conscience, but in her naïve resilience she has reckoned without desire. In practice her new security tempts her to take risks — to try to steal a kiss as she wipes Fernando's lips in full presence of the Court and then to invite him to her chamber in the Duke's absence.

This, the last scene between the lovers (V.1) has some important gaps in the text[7.] which can perhaps be filled in from what they both report of their relations later when under arrest. Bianca is beginning to feel the violation which her marriage and her meeting too late with Fernando have made in her nature. She demands, as Giovanni demands of the Friar, that even now a way may be found for the realisation of her love. She is of course demanding the impossible as Giovanni was not, for she is already committed in conscience, first to her husband and secondly to a compromise which she has agreed upon with Fernando and which she can flout only to her moral and physical danger. It is of this, I believe, that Fernando was intended to remind her in the lost lines. It is evident when the text resumes that he vows not to outlive her should the worst happen — 'that sepulchre that holds Your coffin shall incoffin me alive' (V.l:p.360). It is with an interesting differentiation of character that the lovers now change roles and the tempted becomes the tempter; but the fact is that while Bianca's complexity of temperament can be explained psychologically the credibility of these contrarieties of behaviour is more difficult. There is a Chekhovian element in Bianca's character which titillates the interest but we need to see more of her to believe in her entirely.[8]

What is credible however is the tragic significance of affinity between the lovers, and Ford is at pains to emphasise the point by constantly linking them in service to others about the Court — to Roseilli and Mauruccio, for whom they combine in pleading, and the unfortunate Morona, whose hand they join in marriage to Mauruccio's as the couple leave the Court. In contrast to the Duke's dotage, Fiormunda's lust and Ferentes' debauchery, the force that draws them together is recognition of goodness in one another. Together, and for the brief period in which they are at peace with their conscience, they create an area of stability which is torn apart not only by the machinations of their enemies but also by divisions within themselves. It is unfortunate that the overcrowding of the plot, possibly from the influence of Massinger, prevents not only the full realisation of an unusually complex love relationship but also the development of what might have been one of Ford's most interesting woman characters.

In the final confrontation of the Duke and Bianca, *Othello* is set aside and Bianca's spirited defence, her brutally realistic assessment of her husband's qualities as man and prince, recall the scene of Marcelia's death at the hands of the Duke of Milan, and dominating them both stands Fiormunda. The shaping of this episode is designedly formal; it is Fiormunda's act, her

climax of triumph, and the Duke is her puppet. But he is also
her agent in revenge and it is perhaps intentional that Bianca
seems unaware of her presence. Fiormunda describes herself as
'insphered above' like an avenging goddess, that she may
'cross the race of love despised and triumph' (V.1:p.359).
Momentarily Fiormunda possesses the Duke, it is Fiormunda
who kills Bianca through him but it is the Duke who learns
from the experience. In contrast Fiormunda remains detached
and untouchable, a *dea ex machina*, a character only in
outline, but a type-figure of developing power.

The confusion between the false and the true, between
dream and reality reaches its climax here when the Duke meets
a Bianca whom the shock of discovery has stripped of childish
optimism. It is this new maturity that we hear in her quiet
statement —

> You told me you had dreamt; and gentle Duke
> Unless you be mistook you're now awake —
>
> (V.1:p.361)

and from this point onwards Bianca's part in the dialogue is
the voice of reality. Step by step she shows the Duke the
misapprehensions on which he has built his personal life and
the true value and nature of the love he has professed for her,
and with all this the fact that since he is no valiant hero
violence will not become him:

> Alas good man, put up, put up: thine eyes
> Are likelier much to weep than arms to strike —

an assertion which he proves when a few lines later he drops
his sword.

The treatment of this episode is typically late Jacobean.
Othello is moved to strangle Desdemona suddenly lest her
distress at Cassio's supposed death should distort his motive.
In making the Duke stab Bianca while taking her hand in a
loving gesture Ford is of course repeating himself. It is thus
that Giovanni stabs Annabella and Orgilus will kill Ithocles
with a similar gesture in *The Broken Heart*. But the lengthy
revelatory dialogue, the slow dawning of the truth, recall
from *The Maid's Tragedy* of Beaumont and Fletcher the scene

in which Evadne discloses to Amintor the King's real motive in arranging their marriage, and several episodes of protracted revelation in Middleton's later plays.[9] The emphasis here is two-fold and at first sight contradictory — on the brutal face of fact but also on the courtesy appropriate to a just vengeance. No Elizabethan and few Caroline dramatists would write like this.

The next confrontation is with Fernando, but before the Duke enters the latter has had time to convince Nebrassa and Petruchio of his own and Bianca's innocence. Upon this the Duke's display of the dagger smoking with Bianca's blood is surely deliberately planned. The same audience had no doubt seen *'Tis Pity She's a Whore*, and perhaps fairly recently. For them as for most readers and commentators Giovanni's dagger would create an emotional effect for which the play is still remarkable after more than three centuries. The association would be inevitable and Ford knew he could count upon it. Here as in the previous tragedy, since in both cases the victim is technically innocent, the bloody dagger is a symbol of violation, the Duke's last attempt to justify a love which had no basis in reality, a violation to which all the travesties of love in the play have contributed. It is also the climax of the Duke's obsession with the idea of ripping open the human exterior — 'unrip that womb of bloody mischief (IV.1), 'Rip up the cradle of thy cursed womb' (V.1) — anything to find out the truth, a discovery which he believes he now holds in his hand:

> Look here, 'tis written on my poniard's point,
> The bloody evidence of thy untruth.

> (V.2:p.366)

In fact he finds that it is the evidence of his own mistakings throughout the action: 'Bianca chaste! ... Whither now shall I run from the day?'

However Bianca's 'chastity' may look to a modern age, unquestionably Ford intends us to recognise the love between Bianca and Fernando as the only true relationship in a corrupt environment. The basis of the play casts certain doubts upon the Platonic idealism in which they try to clothe it, but the overall attitude is entirely objective. Moral assessment, approval or blame, is not Ford's purpose[10] nor do the reversals in the last half of the play distance the characters from our sympathy. It is true that the principal characters are victims of their own illusions, that their illusions are concerned with love at their various levels and that all the lovers experience bitter disenchantment when the facts of their situation come upon them. Mauruccio, who had hoped to win a princess, leaves the Court in rags with an elderly whore for his bride, Ferentes, carefree and confident in seduction, is mauled to death by his once lovesick victims, Fiormunda, who had intended to punish Fernando for his rejection of her by inciting the Duke to vengeance, finds him as high in favour as ever, Roseilli, who plays the fool to obtain Fiormunda, finds at the end of the play that she is not worth having. Yet to interpret the play as an ironic exposure of the follies and dangers of passionate love is to distort the experience it is meant to convey. Professor Stavig would have us take Fernando's death by his own hand in Bianca's tomb as the ultimate touch of irony and Fernando himself as an example of passion carried to excess — 'passion crased'.[11]

Are we really expected to believe this? Did Ford really expect his audience to sit through five acts without identifying with any of the main characters? After the revelations in the first part of Act V he had virtually nothing more to say. But the Tourneuresque finale, the open tomb discovering the lover in his shroud, a phial of poison in his hand, preparing to join his true bride in death, was the sort of climax private theatre audiences had grown accustomed to expect in romantic tragedy of revenge. As the only just man in the centre of the play, Fernando can make his tragic assertion of a right to his love, if only in death; equally acceptable, though true in a deeper sense than he can understand, is the Duke's complaint that in anticipating the suicide he himself intended at his wife's tomb, Fernando has cheated him of 'a glorious name'. The final episode may be partly a concession to the theatre, yet it has its use in demonstrating visually Fernando's ultimate dominance in a relationship from which the Duke's own follies have excluded him.

Love's Sacrifice is in every sense a theatre play. Most of the major roles offer scope for originality; the play abounds in confrontations in which two or more characters play upon one another and where the text often seems designed to leave a good deal to the individual actor's interpretation, and the main episodes with their formality or spectacle invite experimental production. Yet on the whole Ford seems to have demanded no more, other than small, transportable properties and furnishings, than the permanent stage fixtures at the Phoenix. These he used with imagination and economy.[12] All the 'discovery' scenes — Fernando's bedchamber, Bianca's closet and the tomb — were probably managed with the cross-stage hangings. Bianca 'draws a curtain and Fernando is discovered in bed sleeping', and when she leaves the stage 'the scene closes' (II.4). The lovers are 'discovered' (V.1) while Fiormunda makes her dramatic entrance above and probably move forward into her line of vision before the Duke's entrance at one of the side doors. From this point, as has become Ford's habit in this play, upper and lower stage communicate, although Bianca seems unaware of Fiormunda's presence. The effect is largely visual; after her moment of irresponsibility Bianca is trapped and the episode vibrates with the excitement of unanswered questions. It is again with the use of the upper stage that Ford turns farce into irony when the Duke and his company observe from the 'gallery above' while Mauruccio practises his amorous posturing (II.2). Not even Marston used the upper stage with greater theatrical effect.[13]

In the final scene, when a church is 'discovered', the stage directions are elaborate but quite explicit. The scene opens to reveal a church 'with a tomb in the background'. Clearly the hangings open at this point and a number of properties must have been previously arranged behind them, probably during the preceding passage of dialogue in an 'apartment in the palace', evidently down stage with the hangings closed, for D'Avolos, being barred from his official place in the 'solemnity', resolves: 'here I will stand to fall amongst 'em in the rear.' It is possible that the central double doors were also utilised to give depth to the church scene, the two doors being folded back against the stage wall.[14] This would demand careful lighting, perhaps with candelabra and stands. Some scenery, perhaps a cloth painted in perspective, may also have been used. The staging of *Love's Sacrifice* seems to build up to this final elaboration, outdoing even the closing scene of *The Broken Heart*; Ford is too practical a theatre-man to overburden his stage-hands who have to prepare for this ultimate and highly important display. From first to last he evidently thought out this play in terms of what the theatre in which it was to be performed could offer.

Clumsiness and irrelevance are customary criticisms of Ford's handling of his sub-plots, especially those written for light relief.[15] This is, I think, a misreading of the sub-plots in general, and particularly those in this play. Their functional significance in reflecting upon and contrasting with the main plot has been commented upon, but the episodes from this minor material are so carefully and regularly spaced that the act divisions become recognisable stages in acceleration. There is every indication that Ford had conceived the secondary plots with the utmost care and with a clearly planned dramatic purpose. Ford's problem is that here and elsewhere the significance of his secondary material, however trivial, however theatrical it may be at first impact, is basically thematic in intention, and in a canvas at once so narrow and so crowded as this it is easy to lose sight of it without more guidance than Ford's natural reticence will permit him to give us. Ford's determination not to do the audience's work for them is a distinguishing feature which nevertheless adds to the difficulty of interpretation. The function of the sub-plots in *Hamlet, King Lear* and *The Changeling* is superficially obvious from their parallelism with the main interest. Here attentiveness in the audience combined with sensitivity in the actors is a necessity if the secondary material is to have its dramatic effect; it is an audience-and-actor partnership which can be fully realised only in small and intimate theatre.

As I have suggested above, the gulf in spirit and content between the play from which he clearly borrowed and that which the plot of *Love's Sacrifice* resembles in outline sets up a division at the basis of Ford's own conception which is never quite reconciled. Up to the climax of the murder of Ferentes Ford seems unable to decide whether he is following the pattern of *Othello* or that of *The Duke of Milan*, and until Bianca's capitulation in the bedchamber scene it is far from clear whether the dramatic interest is to centre like that in *Othello* upon the relationship between husband and wife or upon that between the wife and a lover. Again Ford's arbitrary distinction between adultery and disloyalty raises a fine question in ethics. Moreover the insistence upon Bianca's innocence in the closing scenes is palpably in contradiction both to what she appears to be proposing to Fernando in the discovery scene and to her own plain statement to the Duke before her death. Clearly her innocence is subject to considerable modification. It is a confusion of thinking which makes nonsense of the heroic posturing at the opened tomb.

The relationship between Roseilli and Fiormunda which runs like a thread from beginning to end of the play is again unspecified and undeveloped. Fiormunda's malice towards her suitor has neither motive nor foundation and appears to be no more than a plot device. After the lengths to which he is driven, ostensibly to win her, Roseilli's exploitation of her status and rejection of her as a wife would be chilling if it were not totally unreal. It is in this hesitancy, this unsureness of purpose that the play falls short of greatness.

Why did Ford choose to revise the *Othello* theme and finally what did he make of it? It is clear that he saw Othello's problems in terms of a psychological complexity, but he would not have endorsed the view that it is precisely Othello's nobility of character that makes him easy game to the unscrupulous. To Ford a man can be 'wrought' only if he is weak, and he sees the dangers of weakness primarily in those who bear rule and influence. Nor, I think, would he have believed that innocence such as Desdemona's, however untried, could make even a young wife vulnerable to misconception. Hence perhaps his combination in Bianca of a child-like innocence which can carry her unscathed through malice and envy, and a woman's divided heart. Nor would he accept that a man so oblivious of anything that could be laid to his blame could become an object of suspicion. So Fernando is conceived as an older, wiser man than Cassio, but a great deal more susceptible to passion. Finally the emphasis is not on jealousy, nor on a great mind 'perplexed', but on the fallibility, the contradictoriness, the self-delusion that beset the most dangerous of all passions, sexual love. So for the tragic grandeur of *Othello* Ford has substituted the conflicts that torment the mediocre in positions of power. *Love's Sacrifice* is essentially a play about princes; that it does not stand comparison with *Othello* is partly explicable by its profound difference in scope and attitude to character.

In the study of human self-delusion *Love's Sacrifice* goes a
long way beyond *'Tis Pity*, yet it is to some degree a parody of
that play as well as a comment upon it. Giovanni was typical
of the lover who knows his way in life and has the conviction
to adhere to it. Giovanni sought to reach the heart in order to
justify his stance in morals and in love. Here the search, with
the violence in which it ends, is for truth, not of values but of
what people really are, and the figurative insistence upon
digging, stripping and tearing suggests an ironic comment on
the previous play.[16] Ford's final assertion is that those who
experience passion are likely to resemble Annabella rather
than Giovanni — an interesting suggestion that the problem
of *'Tis Pity She's a Whore* could be reviewed from a different
angle. In this play Ford's sympathy is obviously with Bianca's
uncertainties rather than with Fernando's conviction,
however tragic in the traditional sense such a character as
Fernando may be.

Now this is a new departure in tragedy and an interesting
modification of the typical Jacobean tragic conception. Ford's
interest in the divided mind may owe something to
Middleton's choice of the mediocre character, the confused
rather than the tempted or self-betrayed man, as the centre of a
new kind of tragic experience. But the scope of Middleton's
drama was something Ford was neither able nor willing to
attempt. *Love's Sacrifice* stands many re-readings but one
emerges from it as from the narrow mazes of a sixteenth-
century Italian palace. At every turn there is something of
interest, often something new or strange, but the corridors are
confining, the air oppressive. If, as seems possible, *The Broken
Heart* followed *Love's Sacrifice* it was perhaps natural that
Ford should turn to another Prince's Court, but in a larger,
more orderly setting — that of the classical tragic pattern in the
pure air of Sparta.

5 Return to Blackfriars and the Classical Tragic Pattern in *The Broken Heart*

Whatever the reasons for Ford's brief return to Blackfriars with *The Broken Heart* this play, often regarded as his masterpiece, marks a climax in his work[1]. Again, superficially, Ford gives the Caroline audience what it expects. Here again is the theme of true love wrenched apart by the tyranny of ambition, again we have the conflict between passion and honour, again the tensions of jealousy; again too we have the never-failing joke of the elderly jealous husband and the indifferent young wife. The stage is set for the usual romantic tragedy of frustrated love with a spice of light entertainment. In fact the play implies a criticism more searching than in either of the two previous tragedies of Platonic idealism and conventional ethics, while its restraint in manner and comparative simplicity in staging until the last episode are a rebuke to Caroline theatrical extravagance.

The Broken Heart challenges the whole concept of traditional Revenge Tragedy. Here no character acts alone; the logic of cause and effect is never forgotten, but the trials and ambitions of individuals are absorbed into the pattern of destiny and the moral sanctions are not only those which apply between one man and another, but rather those which ensure the safety and well-being of a whole community. The action of *The Broken Heart* is played out not within the narrow confines either of a Prince's Court or of an urban society but on the stage of the civilised world — between Sparta and Athens, Argos and Delphi. The conflict in which the main characters are engaged is not with a few power-seekers in a restricted circle, but with the ironies of the human condition; and it is bounded and controlled by the will of the gods themselves.

A distinction has often been noted between the outlook of classical tragedy, where divine justice is never questioned and the characters 'stride to their fierce disasters in the grip of truths more intense than knowledge',[2] and that of Elizabethan

79

tragedy which challenges us with unresolved problems. In
The Broken Heart there is bitter protest but the end of the play
leaves us with a sense of acceptance, a recognition of forces
beyond the characters themselves, which they do not attempt
to understand but whose justice they acknowledge. Now this
fundamental affinity with the attitude of Greek tragedy and
the action of the play follows a pattern not unlike that of the
Oresteia.

Here as in the *Agamemnon*, the first of the Aeschylean
trilogy, a wrong has been done in the past between two
families and an act of injustice sparks off the play. Ithocles has
revoked the will of his father Thrasus, which the King himself
has approved, that the feud between his family and that of
Crotolon should be healed by the marriage of his sister
Penthea to Crotolon's son Orgilus. Instead he has satisfied his
own ambition by revoking the marriage contract and forcing
her into marriage with Bassanes, a wealthy nobleman whom
she cannot love and who appears to be impotent. In the
Agamemnon the curse upon the house of Atreus, resulting
from the feud with that of Thyestes, prompts Agamemnon to
sacrifice his daughter to the gods — and to his ambition — in
order to ensure the success of his expedition to Troy, thus
arousing a mother's fury in his wife, Clytemnestra. In both
plays the avenger awaits the return of the successful hero from
the wars to receive honours at home. Having established, like
Ithocles, a right over his sister Euphranea's marriage choice,
Orgilus begs his father's leave to retire to Athens and so
conciliate the jealousy of Bassanes which is tormenting
Penthea. In fact he remains at home disguised as a scholar in
the school of Tecnicus, a philosopher, to wait, as Clytemnestra
waits, and watch events. Meantime his hatred of Ithocles is
enhanced when an alliance grows up between Euphranea and
the close friend of Ithocles, Prophilus.

Ithocles returns beloved and honoured by the old King
Amyclas and acclaimed by his fellows. Like Agamemnon's in
a similar situation his reaction is at first moderate and
generous but, again like Agamemnon, he is tempted to *hubris*.
The Princess Calantha greets him with a provincial garland
woven with her own hands and, as Agamemnon is prevailed
upon by Clytemnestra to walk upon the sacred purple, so
Ithocles is gradually drawn into a passion for the Princess — a

piece of over-reaching which adds fuel to Orgilus' determination upon revenge. At this point Orgilus throws off his disguise and returns to Court where he is presented to the King by Ithocles who now, bitterly regretting his former action, seeks to make amends. Like Clytemnestra welcoming Agamemnon, Orgilus feigns a regard he cannot feel but like Agamemnon Ithocles notices nothing of the irony behind the flattery, for he is bemused both by his own change of heart and by the prospect of a new happiness opening before him. Whereupon, under family pressure, Orgilus drops his opposition to Euphranea's marriage to Prophilus, thus increasing his hold upon Ithocles who like Agamemnon is now completely off guard.

Meantime the action reaches a new phase in the arrival of Nearchus Prince of Argos, a cousin of the Princess and a suitor for her hand. But Calantha is already drawn to Ithocles, who confides his passion to his sister, who reveals it to the Princess. In a charming episode Calantha tosses a ring, which Nearchus has begged, towards Ithocles, who is not slow to pick it up and re-present it to Calantha, who jestingly bestows it upon him. The inevitable courtiers' quarrel ensues but Ithocles is buoyed up with happiness and Nearchus, understanding the situation and seeing that it is acceptable to the King, generously withdraws his suit to make way for the true lovers.

At this turning-point in the action the play again resembles the *Agamemnon*, for like Agamemnon's triumphant entrance into his palace where he will meet his death, this is the moment of apparent joy at which everything begins to decline. The King's health begins to fail, and looking to Calantha's marriage as a means of renewal in the State he consults the oracle at Delphi, instructing Tecnicus to interpret it, only to discover that is prophesies the doom of the dynasty. Tecnicus is the voice of Cassandra/Tiresias prophesying doom and then withdrawing into death or obscurity. Tecnicus' last act is to warn both young men of coming disaster: to Ithocles, 'the lifeless trunk shall wed the broken heart', and to Orgilus, 'revenge proves its own executioner', and he leaves the stage as Cassandra leaves it in the *Agamemnon*, with ominous words — 'O Sparta, O Lacedoemon!' There follows the second decline in the scene of Penthea's derangement with her subsequent death, so that at the summit of his happiness the

evil that Ithocles has done in the past comes to fruition and the
time is ripe for retribution.

Like Agamemnon caught and killed in Clytemnestra's net
as she pretends to perform the duty of a wife at the bath,
Ithocles after being courteously led by Orgilus to Penthea's
death chamber, is trapped in the mechanical chair which
Orgilus has prepared for him and there stabbed to death.
Meantime the dance at Euphranea's wedding is in full swing
and it is in the course of it that Calantha hears the news first of
her father's death, then of Penthea's and lastly of the murder of
Ithocles, all of which she receives apparently unmoved,
continuing the measure until the dance is completed. Like
Clytemnestra, Orgilus freely admits the murder and like her he
dies for it. Calantha's first act on assuming her reign as Queen
is to sentence him to death and at his request, by his own hand.
So revenge becomes 'its own executioner'.

Calantha herself, who has the greatest loss to bear, receives
Orgilus' confession with a phrase which stops short of rebuke
— 'You have done it?' — and delivers her sentence with the
cold detachment of an absolute justice. Calantha has assumed
the role of a goddess — a *dea ex machina* — rather than a
sovereign. But the close of the play has something in common
with the intervention of Athena in the final episode of the
Oresteia, in order to reconcile the Eumenides who are
hounding Orestes for killing his mother, Clytemnestra, in
revenge for his father's death. Here the final scene presents the
coronation of Calantha with the dead Ithocles lying crowned
at her side. The ceremony over, Calantha settles the Kingdom
upon Nearchus, not only reviving the State of Sparta but also
healing the grief-torn individuals by giving each one a
responsibility and a destiny that cancel out their guilt.
Although there is of course no direct parallel, this episode,
with its clear statement and unemotional treatment, is in the
spirit of the release from guilt of the tormented Orestes and the
transformation of the Eumenides into a blessing on the city
which they were intended to curse. Calantha's 'new-wedding'
of Ithocles with her mother's wedding ring is the signal of her
own death, for with it she gives tongue at last to the 'silent
griefs' which have cut her own 'heart strings'. So the 'lifeless
trunk' has wedded the 'broken heart' — 'Those that are dead

Are dead' and Sparta is entering upon a new and healthier phase of growth. As at the close of the *Oresteia*, the evil is wound up.

I do not suggest that Ford was consciously imitating the *Agamemnon* or any other classical Greek tragedy, but the similarities in pattern and development are interesting enough to indicate a new direction of thinking. This dispassionate treatment of a just retribution was new to Ford as it was new to Jacobean and to Caroline tragedy and in this connection the conception of fate in this play is worth noting. In *'Tis Pity* and *Love's Sacrifice* a man's destiny was written in his own qualities of mind and temperament. Here fate is determined by the will of the gods and as has been shown the play's resolution turns upon Tecnicus' interpretation of the oracle at Delphi. The gods alone are 'privy' to the secrets of the heart, the eyes of the gods are 'quick-piercing'. The gods are 'moderators', the gods' 'witness', and in the last lines of the play the preceding events are seen as the 'effects' of 'the counsels of the gods'. This insistence upon forces beyond the scope of human life which they clearly determine is peculiar to this play and will be translated in terms of history in *Perkin Warbeck*.

That Ford was trying to forge a new tragic pattern is suggested, I think, by the manner of the exposition in the opening scene. His usual practice is to plunge us straight into the main issues of the play — as in Giovanni's challenge to the Friar in *'Tis Pity* or Roseilli's protest at his suspension from Court in *Love's Sacrifice*. Here while the play opens with Crotolon's fatherly testiness, considerable space is given to Orgilus' résumé of wrongs done in the distant and more immediate past, between his own family and that of Thrasus, facts which are perfectly familiar to Crotolon. This expository scene has something of the effect of a Greek opening chorus; it is acceptable on that level while, as Joan Sargeaunt notes, it draws attention to the gradual working of a poison, which later Crotolon calls an 'infection', in the mind of Orgilus.[3] Ford has chosen to sacrifice naturalism in order to stress in the returning hero, whom we meet in the following scene, a crime against humanity, now in the past but to be increasingly remembered in the ensuing action.

There is a similar formality and an unwonted simplicity in
the shape of the plot as a whole. Here for the first time Ford
dispenses with a comic sub-plot and distinctions of major and
minor among the central characters would not be easy. Here
are three couples — Orgilus and Penthea, Prophilus and
Euphranea, Ithocles and Calantha — paired according to their
natures, who should have revolved in perfect harmony round
their King, Amyclas. It is an intimate circle resembling a close-
knit family rather than a royal Court, for Amyclas is
personally concerned in all their fortunes. Until Calantha's
final settlement we hear nothing of State affairs but we see a
good deal of the king/father's attempts to guide Euphranea
and Prophilus, Calantha and Ithocles towards their
happiness. The ideal Court of Sparta is summed up in
Ithocles' application of the image of the dance to moral action:

> Morality applied
> To timely practice, keeps the soul in tune
> At whose sweet music all our actions dance.[4]
>
> (II.2:p.212)

Ithocles is speaking of the harmony within the soul of the
individual, but the visual use of the dance later suggests rather
the harmony within the small community of the Spartan
Court and beyond that the safe government of the State, which
the pride and ambition of Ithocles have disturbed. He has
himself introduced the discordant element in the jealous and
ageing Bassanes, so that Penthea and Orgilus are wrenched
apart and his own and his sister's natures divided against
themselves — their souls out of 'tune'. It is in the context of
this balanced dance that Calantha's refusal to have the
measure interrupted by reported evils should be read.
Calantha is the ordering principle in the play. When she
makes her own marriage choice, not for advantage but for love,
she cancels out Ithocles' fault and it is Calantha's death,
without protest and with a constructive acceptance of the
situation, that frees the State for a new beginning.

The quasi-allegorical nature of the theme is slightly borne
out by the symbolic names of the main characters:
Nearchus (new prince), Orgilus (angry), Ithocles (honour of

loveliness), Penthea (complaint), Calantha (flower of beauty), Bassanes (vexation). None of this amounts to more than a framework, but noted in Ford's character list it draws attention to the course of the action and goes some way towards defining the meaning of the play. For within this framework Ford has built up a psychological analysis of character and motive more penetrating and more varied than anything in his previous experiments in tragedy.

Many critics see Penthea as the centre of interest,[5] but the plight of a young woman forced into marriage against her heart and honour is only one of the play's themes and in fact the opening scenes focus attention rather upon Ithocles. Orgilus' bitter complaint against him defines him as proud, ambitious and revengeful, a climber and a bully who has used his sister for his own ends by 'cunning' and 'threats'. But while the Court awaits him in the following scene, we hear, in flat contradiction to the opinion of Orgilus, 'with what moderation, Calmness of nature, measure, bounds and limits Of thankfulness and joy' he takes his success — an impression which is amply confirmed when he appears in person by his modest bearing and generous recognition of the achievements of lesser men. Evidently then, there are two conflicting natures in Ithocles, nor is he spared when, after this triumphant return he witnesses the misery of Penthea in the thraldom to which he has committed her. When we meet him next he is struggling with some grief as yet undefined, but he has learnt the fallibility of ambition when it 'strives to perch on clouds'. When later Crotolon reproaches him, Ithocles freely admits the wrong he did but his excuse is significant — he did not then know 'the secrets of commanding love'. Ithocles begins to emerge as the world's hero, conditioned by success and consequent power, suddenly faced with a new kind of challenge which strips him of his defences. The Ithocles we see in the episode with Penthea (III.2) is a man on the deathbed of his old self, without a new self to put in its place. Like the 'seeled dove' of his soliloquy (II.2:p.212) that has mounted too high he feels himself tumbling 'headlong down with heavier ruin'.

In this scene, one of the loveliest in Ford's plays, Ithocles faces the actual human consequences of his own crime against

his sister, effects which he himself is now experiencing in what
he believes to be a hopeless passion for the Princess:

> My rash spleen
> Hath with a violent hand plucked from thy bosom
> A love-blest heart to grind it into dust
> For which mine's now a-bleeding.
>
> (III.2:p.227)

The last line quoted implies less an expression of penitence
than a shared experience. There follows a duet, not unlike the
classical *commos* and recalling *The Lover's Melancholy*
(IV.3:p.72) in which the speakers mingle their sorrows in a
nostalgic meditation on the simple life of peasants. Penthea is
moved but she will not yield. He has betrayed their name to
infamy for he has made of her 'a spotted whore' in the 'known
adultery' of her marriage with Bassanes, and Ithocles admits
that the event has made his actions 'monstrous'. For Ithocles
the process of self-knowledge is a reversal.

The development of Ithocles projects as a major interest
here a theme recurrent in the tragedies — the confusion
between the false and the true. His return to Sparta, to
Penthea and her unhappiness, to Calantha and the impact of
his love, has shown him the hollowness of the values which
have guided him hitherto. Thenceforth Ithocles becomes a
seeker after truth, the real, visible, material happiness which
for all his success has so far eluded him. Three times his desires
are associated with clouds: once in the soliloquy quoted above,
in which he sees his ambition blindly perching on clouds;
next in Bassanes' taunt that vanity has reared his name up to
'bestride a cloud' (III.2:p.230) and again when Armostes warns
him that 'Ixion aiming To embrace Juno bosom'd but a cloud'
(IV.1:p.247). It is worth noting that when his reconciliation
with Penthea frees him from the burden of guilt to take the
initiative, his actions are all on the level of practical
effectiveness. He takes his sister into his own protection
against her husband's jealousy, enquires in the mad scene
when she slept last (while Orgilus cares only for her state of
mind), goes out of his way to do a service to Orgilus (whose
friendship, in his new-found confidence, he too readily

assumes), is swift to retrieve Calantha's ring and is as defiant as a schoolboy when the gesture is resented. This unreflective if straightforward behaviour of Ithocles, which perturbs his older colleagues, is a foil to the darker designs of Orgilus, but it is none the less that which the Greeks regarded as a madness visited by the gods upon the doomed. After leading and presumably assessing other men, he is blind to the sinister irony of Orgilus' flattery; he is indeed the 'seeled dove' mounting dangerously and blindly.

In an important speech to Armostes, Ithocles contrasts the dreams of worldly felicity with the tangible happiness of waking sense:

> Their very dreams present 'em choice of pleasures,
> Pleasures — observe me uncle — of rare object;
> Here heaps of gold, there increments of honours,
> Now change of garments, then the votes of people;
> Anon varieties of beauties, courting,
> In flatteries of the night, exchange of dalliance:
> Yet these are still but dreams. Give me felicity
> Of which my senses waking are partakers,
> A real visible, material happiness.
>
> (IV.1:p.247)

We shall meet the confrontation of dream and reality in Penthea's last appearance; for the moment these lines mark an important stage in Ithocles' self-realisation. He has discovered the true sources of self-fulfilment, but his vision is limited, so that the radiance of his discovery blinds him to everything but itself. For the time being obstacles crumble before him. The King's favour, Calantha's response, the withdrawal of Nearchus, conspire to secure his suit and Ithocles is ravished with the promise of it. But although the audience may not doubt the sincerity of this love it is clear that many characters in his own circle do. In the context of Armostes' warning, the taunts of Amelus, the follower of Nearchus, and the irony of Orgilus, all of which he ignores, Ithocles' motives have an apparent ambiguity to which, in contrast to his previous self-analysis, he is now entirely oblivious. But I think Professor Stavig is mistaken in interpreting the speech quoted above as evidence of an interest in acquiring material possessions 'which he now lacks'.[6] The word 'material' is open to several interpretations. Ithocles is talking about reality and a few lines earlier he speaks scornfully of those who dream — surely in the sense of daydreaming or brooding, as he himself has done in the past — of worldly possessions and delights as the true objectives of living, nor is there any evidence in the play that he 'lacks' means. Ithocles' 'material happiness' is in direct opposition to Armostes' figure of a man bosoming a cloud; in the context it underlines the idea of the tangible and lasting which Ithocles yearns for. But to emphasise either side of Ithocles' nature is to lose sight of the complexity of human motive and reaction on which the play is built. This is the heart of the problem which Ithocles now faces; he has substituted pride of life, *hubris*, for the earlier pride of ambition, his mood is dangerous and like some other central characters he finds reality too late. It is this dichotomy at the basis of the conception of Ithocles that motivates the play — the force of passion behind two disparate obsessions, ambition and love. There is a remarkable reticence in the handling of this character in the middle scenes; the delineation is vivid but it is like a silent film without a commentary. The inference is that Ithocles has never entirely reconciled the division in himself and cannot do so until he finds the 'long-looked-for peace' of death.

The vengeance which pursues Ithocles is two-handed. First Penthea, then Orgilus is the agent, but it is Penthea who inflicts the deepest wound, for in her betrothal to Orgilus Penthea was to have been the means of healing the feud between their two families; in fact by Ithocles' action she has become the cause of further division.

Penthea has no need to seek for truth, for she embodies the absolute of integrity itself and she moves through the play like a searing flame. With Penthea there are no half-measures, no compromise; contracted by Orgilus she is his wife in spirit and any other union is a violation. Her forced marriage to Bassanes is to her a rape, but Lucrece's knife cannot save her, for her soul is 'leprous' from the 'known adultery' in which she is compelled to live. Penthea dies from within.[7] Her attitude is clarified when Orgilus, disguised as a scholar, confronts her in the garden, for later in derangement she specifically refers to this episode:

> When we last gathered roses in the garden
> I found my wits; but truly you lost yours.

(IV.2:p.255)

The rose symbolises the perfection they both seek, but their quest is in sharply contrasting ways. While Orgilus pleads for some compromise with the situation — that he may 'possess' his wife — Penthea clearly sees that their love can never be consummated even should she outlive her 'bondage'. Penthea's standards of chastity and honour are daunting but she does not evade, as Orgilus tries to, the reality of their consequences. To give him comfort she reaffirms her faith by the ceremonial handclasp at which they both kneel, but she as readily turns upon him in fierce anger when passion drives him to importunity. He has lost his wits but in the same moment, in a flash of comprehension which clarifies her future action, she finds hers. Again, some lines from the mad scene illumine this episode:

> tis a fine deceit
> To pass away in a dream; indeed I've slept
> With mine eyes open a great while.

(IV.2:p.253)

Penthea's realism is as relentless as her integrity; Orgilus may pass away his life in a dream either of revenge or of the fulfilment of love — the one as unreal as the other, Ithocles may lose himself in a fantasy of perfect happiness with Calantha, but Penthea does not dream. Her life may be no more than a sleep but her eyes are open. For Penthea the situation in which Ithocles has placed them all, either directly or through the effect of his actions on near associates, must be faced and lived through.

Ford's habit of stripping the traditional moral code down to its roots is seen with peculiar force in Penthea and more credibly than in Giovanni. Neither the ceremony of marriage nor the accepted view of society can alter the fact that Penthea

is living under a mortal sin which permanently stains her
honour, the 'real honour' of Tecnicus which does not depend
upon 'opinion'. By carrying it to extremes in Penthea, Ford
explodes the neo-Platonic idea of the love of true hearts as he
will that of conventional honour and loyalty in *The Lady's
Trial*. *The Broken Heart* takes us a long way beyond the
teachings of a coterie or for that matter of a code of ethics.

It is this ruthless reality that Penthea compels Ithocles to
face when she visits him alone in his sickness of mind. Her first
move is to drag him back from the womb-nostalgia of his wish
that he had died in the cradle, to look upon that 'sin of life'
which he committed in violating his dead father's wishes, nor
does she allow him to evade the issue by indulging in
protestations of penitence; he must feel the effects of it in
himself and see them in her. When finally she makes him
reveal the 'saint' he serves and learns that his hopeless state
matches her own, Penthea forces him to consider the
possibility of Calantha being married away from him, as she
has been from her own lover, to the Prince of Argos. But it is at
this point, where she has humbled his pride and has him in her
power, that the healer in Penthea emerges. For Penthea is no
mere instrument of a darker kind of vengeance; Penthea cuts to
the heart but she wounds to make new —

> We are reconciled ...
> 'tis not fit we should divide;
> Have comfort, you may find it —

(III.2:p.230)

and like her brother she seeks for the practical — 'means,
speedy means and certain' — in her determination to 'cheer
invention for an active strain'. In retrospect this reconciliation
colours the whole episode between Ithocles and Penthea with
a gentleness the more impressive for the sharp integrity of
Penthea's handling of it. This is compassion without the
overflow of feeling which sometimes muddies the issue in the
plays of Beaumont and Fletcher and their followers. It is part
of a womanliness which continually tempers the corrosive
qualities of Penthea's character and role in the play. When
Bassanes breaks in upon her colloquy with Ithocles and a duel

nearly ensues, it is Penthea who takes charge of the situation
with the dignity of a mature woman and a wife —

> With favour let me speak. My lord what slackness
> In my obedience hath deserved this rage?...
>
> (III.2:p.232)

and both contestants are silenced.

Like Ithocles Penthea grows within the action. Between the
melancholy resignation of her first appearance and the barbed
utterances which anticipate her physical collapse, the
integrity of her convictions — a sort of innocence —
strengthens her spirit as she passes from one encounter to
another and it is this newly-realised maturity that prompts
her skilful handling of the Princess when she pleads with her
for Ithocles. In laying before her listener the image of her own
desolation in the fanciful last will, Penthea penetrates the
'castle of the mind' in the royal Princess in order to prepare her
for the final bequest of her brother's love. Her purpose is of
course to bring Calantha to recognise, as she has made Ithocles
recognise, the true state of her feelings through emotional
shock. Her approach is therapeutic and her last lines leave an
impression of extreme fatigue:

> My reckonings are made even; death or fate
> Can now nor strike too soon nor force too late.
>
> (III.5:p.244)

It is strange that Clifford Leech should have construed these
lines as an intimation of revenge and her intervention with
Calantha on Ithocles' behalf as an attempt to involve him in a
dangerous ambition.[8] Surely the 'reckonings' are benign;
Penthea has restored the balance so that the happiness of
Ithocles and Calantha will cancel out the misery of Orgilus
and Penthea. She has played her part and the rest is now for
forces beyond her; it is these suprahuman forces, the will of the
gods, that seem to inspire her in her derangement.

The mad scene should be read in the light of Orgilus'
assertion that some 'minister of fate' has unseated Penthea's
reason. All that she says and does in this scene is prophetic,
either in revelation or in foresight; it is a remarkably succinct

summary of what the play has been about so far and also of
Penthea's own experience. As the mouthpiece of the gods her
vision of the persons in the play as Sirens who sing 'one
another's knell' is apt, for Penthea's fate is the first of a series of
deaths, all interdependent — Penthea, Ithocles, Orgilus,
Calantha, in logical sequence. Her frustrated motherhood of
'many pretty, prattling babes', her insistence upon herself as a
'ravished wife Widowed by lawless marriage', suggest that
Bassanes' reference to an 'outrage' for which he asks
forgiveness is more than the jealousy he has shown
throughout the play. Since Ford had already written a play on
the theme of incest and would write another bearing on that of
impotence, it is hardly likely that his reticence here is from fear
of censorship. This hint of a marital outrage lends credibility
to the profound but sudden change that Penthea's condition
sets up in him, without distracting attention from the play's
main interest. Bassanes has been shocked into self-realisation,
his jealous temper finally rebuked and his mind set upon the
achievement of patience. Even so Penthea has a kind word for
him — 'Take comfort; You may live well and die a good old
man' — which is precisely the destiny which lies ahead of him
at the close of the action. It is interesting that the idea of
comfort recurs so frequently in this the most relentless
character in the play.

Penthea's reminder, by the handclasp, of their meeting in
the garden is both a rebuke and a warning to Orgilus. By his
rejection of reality it is he, not she, who is mad; her cry 'Have ye
seen a straying heart?' is an emblematic statement of her own
fate and his, for it evokes the division from faith and truth
which she and Orgilus must suffer in her marriage. Twice
earlier in the play Penthea refers arrestingly to her heart — that
she has lost her heart and lived a long time without it
(III.5:p.242), that there is a divorce between her body and her
heart (II.3:p.219); now her heart is withered and empty — 'all
crannies'. There follow the accusing references to Ithocles.

Admittedly Orgilus' abrupt exit, presumably to prepare for
the murder of Ithocles, might bear out the impression that
Penthea is deliberately inciting him to vengeance. But that
interpretation would destroy the prophetic force of Penthea's
character and reduce the scene of her derangement to a plot
device. 'Too much happiness will make folk proud they say' —

and immediately Ithocles comes to her mind: 'That's he' — the over-proud and dangerously happy. Yet, characteristically, Ford does not allow Penthea's dramatic function to obscure her human credibility. The comment that in contrast to her own predicament Ithocles' heart is safe 'in the cabinet of the princess', the expectation of the true marriage with 'points and bride laces', with the back-references to her rejection of her own lover are all expressive of an unconscious, and natural, envy in a deranged mind; but again there comes the accusing finger — 'That's he and still 'tis he.' As often in the plays, and especially in *The Broken Heart*, Ford emphasises with a visible object what has been implied already in the action. Penthea's pointing finger singles out with compelling clarity the real destroyer of the equilibrium of Amyclas' Court and of the individuals within it, of that integrity of spirit to which 'all our actions dance'. Ithocles has repented, she has aided him to remake his life, but nothing can remove the fact of his past sin. In contrast to that which Orgilus meditates, Penthea's is the just vengeance, for it penetrates deeper than the physical; he has 'paid for it home' already. Like so much of the text in the crisis scenes of the play, the words are ambiguous, but if a warning is intended Ithocles does not hear it and Orgilus, characteristically, misunderstands.

The character of Orgilus, like that of Calantha, is slightly flattened to suit the requirements of his semi-traditional role in the play. Orgilus is the avenger, but there is a freshness about the conception. Almost every word he speaks is forceful and often double-edged, yet he is neither a Vindice nor a male Clytemnestra. He has the avenger's one-track mind, obsessed with the facts as he sees them — that he has been tricked of his love and that his destined bride has been sold into thraldom. So Ithocles and all associated with him are objects of implacable hate. Again Orgilus has the avenger's inclination to continue and propagate the evils of the past; he alone remembers the family feud which the King himself had hoped to see healed in his marriage with Penthea and his desire to have a voice in his sister's marriage choice suggests the prolongation of the sin of Ithocles like a curse. His animosity to Prophilus and determination to hurt Ithocles through his friend and the forcefulness of his asides when he meets Prophilus and Euphranea in his scholar's disguise are some

indication that this was originally intended to be the main
interest.[9] As it stands, the episode defines the uncompromising
nature of Orgilus' anger and his capacity for sheer negation.
Twice he counters, aside, the positive hopes of Prophilus with
a flat denial. When Prophilus expresses himself as already
'sure of Ithocles a friend Firm and unalterable', Orgilus
murmurs 'But a brother more cruel than the grave' (I.3:p.201)
and later when Prophilus invokes the smile of Hymen —
'We'll feed thy torches with eternal fires' — and leaves the
scene in assured happiness, Orgilus breaks his control with

> Put out thy torches Hymen or their light
> Shall meet a darkness of eternal night.

(I.3:p.205)

Already murder is in his thoughts, but in contrast to Vindice
on the one hand and Clytemnestra on the other it is in fact
murder, not a just, if ruthless, retribution either from man or
from destiny. Orgilus embodies the death wish and it is thus
that, on his return to Court, he strives to obstruct the concern
of Amyclas for his subjects' happiness.

As usual Ford leaves a good deal to the prompter and the
actor in the scene in which Orgilus yields to persuasion in the
matter of Euphranea's marriage. If Orgilus is supposed to be
playing a part the text gives no indication of it, but meantime
Ithocles has begun to place himself in Orgilus' power by
proffering what is on his side a sincere friendship. Orgilus'
assessment of precisely what value Ithocles should place on
such a friendship is clear from his comment to Crotolon:

>   lordly Ithocles
> Hath graced my entertainment in abundance,
> Too humbly hath descended from that height
> Of arrogance and spleen which wrought the rape
> On grieved Penthea's purity; his scorn
> Of my untoward fortunes is reclaimed
> Unto a courtship, almost to a fawning:-
> I'll kiss his foot since you will have it so.

(III.4:p.237)

The obvious sarcasm of his greeting to Ithocles 'Most
honoured ever favoured' is a warning of his real attitude, but

the imperviousness of Ithocles to the real situation is matched by Orgilus' inability to feel the emptiness of honour which can be satisfied with acts of violence. The glimpse we have just had into his mind in the lines quoted from the betrothal scene, contrasted with the warmth of his outward behaviour, builds up a suspense which reaches a climax at his offer of a slight device to celebrate the marriage.

Jacobean audiences were well used to 'devices'. or plays within the play as a cover for acts of vengeance; Ford had himself twice employed the device for the same purpose elsewhere. That this anticipation with its accompanying excitement and subsequent surprise is deliberate is borne out by a pointed reference to it as an explanation of the absence of Ithocles and Orgilus from the dance (V.2:p.270). In fact Orgilus does invent a 'device' in the formal triptych of the veiled figure of the dead Penthea seated between the avenger and the victim which is the prelude to Ithocles' death. The total effect of Orgilus' twice-changed plans, without wavering or hesitancy, is to suggest that he too is being used; he is the instrument of forces beyond his knowledge — an impression which a Greek tragic chorus would have made explicit.

Orgilus' obduracy, his failure to understand Penthea's view of their situation, is clarified in his meeting with her in the garden. As he seizes the opportunity to plead with her for their mutual love he declares his own conception of reality in the image of a banquet seen but not as yet enjoyed contrasted with 'the real taste of food' (II.3:p.218). The image stamps the speaker. Orgilus with his 'hungry appetite' is like a starving child outside a pastrycook's window. There is something primitive and earthy about Orgilus. Not for him the confusion between the true and the false that torments Ithocles. His guide to the true is a natural craving; he will break all the rules to possess it and will know it when he tastes it, and he asks as much of Penthea when he urges her — 'I would possess my wife'. Penthea's reply that this would drive her from private to public infamy, that even if she should outlive her 'bondage' the defilement of her false marriage unfits her for the true one, simply bewilders him. To Penthea the affirmation of a love freely given but not to be enjoyed is the only reality left to them. It is his failure to accept this reality that moves her to anger, but the encounter leaves him only the more determined to cut his way through what he does not understand; he will be 'a man resolved to do'.

Orgilus and Penthea do not meet again until the mad scene and here the distinction between them is sharper still. Orgilus can admire valour, as he does when he watches Ithocles die, but the homelier virtues of compassion in Penthea and self-control in the reformed Bassanes elude him. His mockery of Bassanes' new-found patience — his 'whining grey dissimulation' — is as blind as his scorn of Ithocles' joy. Orgilus is not only the avenger, he is also the destroyer, the denial of life's capacity for renewal. It is thus that he takes Penthea's singling out of Ithocles as one who has suffered and may suffer more for the wrongs he has done, as an incitement to action. In the play this is the ultimate miscalculation which makes regeneration impossible except by death.

Reality confronts Orgilus for the first time when, at his death, Ithocles tricks him of half his intention in his act of vengeance. As Irving Ribner observes, Orgilus must kill Ithocles 'because honour demands it, but the manner of the killing demands a total forfeit of honour'[10]. The chair in which he is trapped, in contrast to the net in the *Agamemnon*, which is a symbol of humiliation, is indeed a 'throne of coronation' for Ithocles. He can welcome the dagger which Orgilus draws upon him as an outward sign of the consequences of his own wrongdoing which he accepts and pays for, so that what Orgilus, like Clytemnestra, intended as the ultimate defeat is in fact a triumph; Ithocles has 'cozened' him of honour. Ithocles' 'sacred altar of a long-looked-for peace' on which he sacrifices life and the pride of life foreshadows the altar of Calantha's coronation, where he also will wear the crown. It is significant that in Orgilus' subsequent appearances he shows neither scorn nor anger. Meeting his sentence without protest, he dies by his own hand and with the help of those appointed to see it is carried out, so that his executioners become his friends. The ritualistic element in all three death scenes points to a common implication; like Ithocles, like Calantha in the following scene, Orgilus has learnt acceptance of forces beyond his sphere.

So as the main characters come to terms with themselves the just and the unjust vengeance cancel one another out. As suggested above it is as if the ordering power of Athena has in Sparta, as in Agamemnon's Argos, neutralised the destructive force of the Eumenides. The emblematic nature of the play, to which Stavig draws attention,[11] contributes to a sense of an intention beyond the characters' understanding. The dramatic impressiveness of the visual emblems of death in the three death scenes has been noted. But the ring and the crown are dominant emblems in the action. Calantha's ring which Nearchus begs and Ithocles retrieves and retains has a strong visual effect outweighing what is said in significance; it foreshadows the other ring, bequeathed by the King, which she places on the finger of the dead Ithocles at her coronation, so that the ring becomes symbolic as the action develops, both of marriage and of royalty. The provincial garland which Calantha weaves for Ithocles and presents at his first appearance is an earnest of the royalty he will attain through her love, a royalty which Orgilus continually harps upon in scorn and which will be bestowed upon him in the ultimate irony of his death. The two crowns, of success and of death, are given a strong visual emphasis, the first in the text, the second in the stage directions, nor are we allowed to forget their possible double significance. The emblems in the play have an equivocal implication which Calantha clarifies as Queen, and in this connection Ford's handling of Calantha is an important aspect of his intention.

It is essential that while we accept Calantha as the prospective bride of Ithocles in the half courtly, half humorous business of the ring episode, she remains none the less remote, distanced in the theme of the play. There is no inexplicable hiatus in her development as in that of Bianca in *Love's Sacrifice*, but she betrays no intimacy; there is no soliloquy, no confidence to a friend or attendant. Her sole audible reaction to Penthea's revelation is the aside, following a momentary irritability with her women — 'Ithocles? Wronged Lady!' — which tells us little. The only other glimpse we have into her mind is the aside as she determines to ask the King for the hand of Ithocles — 'Now or never ... have I kept my word?' (IV.3:p.261). The last query contains all that we know of what passed between Ithocles and herself in the gallery. Ford seems to conserve the dramatic force of the character until she can assume her thematic function in the closing scenes where she becomes the outward expression of continence, that discipline of the whole self which can result only from harmony within.

Calantha's suprahuman self-control in the dance, when grief falls upon her in blow after blow, is thus a deliberate exaggeration. As the play ends the patterned movement, implied in Ithocles' dance, of actions of the three couples round their King is to be restored. Euphranea and Prophilus are wedded and the festivities over; Penthea and Orgilus are reunited, Calantha is married to Ithocles — in death: and Bassanes, the discordant element, is removed from their orbit into an active and useful life. 'Those who are dead are dead' — the irony of events has run its course and they have come to terms with it, but Calantha implies that the living still have a destiny to fulfil. In Calantha the counsels of the gods of Nearchus' final couplet are seen to be benign. The attitude goes deeper than stoicism, nor has it anything to do with resignation.[12] It is rather a practical, positive apprehension of the meaning of life and a way of living.

No other tragedy of Ford ends quite like this; here there is no lamenting that never 'here befell a sadder day', no sighing of ''tis pity', but rather a sense of something completed, a circle closed and order restored. The meaning of the play is thus implicit in the pattern of the plot, resolving the tension between the true and the false values in Ithocles, and that between the just and the unjust vengeance which differentiates the dramatic functions of Penthea and Orgilus. In no other play by Ford and in few plays of the period do the construction and the meaning so perfectly cohere — and in few other plays are the characters so completely involved in the tragic experience.

Yet the treatment even of major characters varies considerably in intensity. Professor Kitto notes an essential difference between the concentration in Greek tragedy upon theme without analysis of human motive or moral attitude, and the Elizabethan habit of 'extension' in development of human character and behaviour. The Greek dramatists represented life by a 'rigorous selection', the Elizabethans by 'an inspired aggregation of particulars'.[13] While perhaps nowhere else has Ford explored so thoroughly the springs of human conduct or the interaction of character and situation, there is in *The Broken Heart* a selection which seems to be deliberately planned. Only Ithocles and Penthea are clearly developed in the round; other characters may be vividly or sensitively drawn but they remain figures rather than persons, marked for their dramatic function rather than presented as problems worth resolving in themselves.

There is a similar restraint in the handling of the theme. The violation of a true love is at the core of the play, yet the idea is held at arm's length at the level of abstraction, and romantic interest is at the minimum. It was the effect of passion, not passion itself that was to be the concern in *The Broken Heart*, a distinction which could be salutary in the Caroline theatre, and like the classical dramatists Ford was prepared to jettison a good deal in order to keep his themes clear of extraneous matter.

Here for the first time Ford manages light relief without inventing specifically comic material. Bassanes with his two grumbling servants sparks off humour in his only half-comic jealous obsessions, but still more in his fundamental simplicity. Bassanes is less determined to reform than prone to imagine himself the gentle husband and patient sufferer he would like to be. 'I never gave you one ill word — say did I? Indeed I did not' (III.2:p.232) is his plea to Penthea after the uproar he has made in breaking into her conversation with Ithocles. There is a wry, yet not the less comic irony in his avowed refusal to lose control of his temper under Orgilus' malicious observation in the mad scene, and when Bassanes calls upon the flames of Etna to consume him, Orgilus' comment is more prophetic than he knows — 'Behold a patience ... Do something worth a chronicle' (IV.2:p.254). This is tragic humour, not the light relief of a comic character introduced as a plot device but the friction of one character upon another, each bent, in comic single-mindedness, on his own purpose. It is the humour of a compassionate, but none the less acute observation.

Brian Morris comments in some detail on the variety of language in *The Broken Heart* — from colloquial speech in Bassanes to the poetry of direct statement in which the line is 'vibrant' from its placing in 'the context of utter simplicity', and those meditative passages, 'dream sequences', where the movement of the syntax 'acts as an anodyne upon understanding'.[14] The last characteristic is, I think, one of the chief obstacles to the immediate impact of Ford's greatest work as drama. *The Broken Heart* is musical both in style and conception. The shape of the plot, the sense of movement towards an end within an ordered framework, has something of the discipline of the symphony. Many critics have noted Ford's moments of stillness when the line seems to freeze into silence like a diminuendo in music. Several such passages in this play recall the lyricism of *The Lover's Melancholy*; the dialogue between Ithocles and Penthea (III.2) is an outstanding example. But more important is the sheer music of some of Ford's verse, which nevertheless sometimes diverts the attention from meaning. In such lines the characters seem to meditate within themselves at the expense of outward communication. An unexpected example is in Orgilus' appeal to Penthea in the garden, where the nostalgic tone of the lines, the elaborated imagery surrounding the figure of the Vestal altar and the speaker's involvement with his own thoughts are at variance with the passion he is meant to express:

> turn those eyes
> (The arrows of pure love) upon that fire
> Which once rose to a flame, perfumed with vows
> As sweetly scented as the incense smoking
> On Vesta's altars — virgin tears (like
> The holiest odours) sprinkled dews to feed 'em,
> And to increase their fervour.[15]
>
> (II.3:p.218)

A similar preoccupation lays a weight upon the dialogue for a brief space when Penthea and Ithocles indulge themselves with a dream of the simple life (III.2). Again the effect is musical rather than dramatic; the speakers think alike, not together, and until Penthea breaks the spell by attacking Ithocles they do not communicate. Another typical example is the song which introduces this scene:

> Can you paint a thought? or number
> Every fancy in a slumber? ...
>
> No, oh no! yet you may
> Sooner do both that and this,
> This and that and never miss,
> Than by any praise display
> Beauty's beauty ...
>
> (III.2:p.226)

The heavy monosyllables against the repetitive movement of the lines perhaps took the fancy of G.M. Hopkins, whose *Leaden Echo* may owe something to this lyric. But the difference — and with it a fundamental weakness in Ford — is sharp by comparison. In Hopkins every repetition has its cumulative effect in meaning:

> How to keep ...
> Back beauty, keep it, beauty, beauty, beauty ...
> from vanishing away ...
> No there's none, there's none, O no there's none ...
> So be beginning, be beginning to despair ...

Ford's lines are soporific while Hopkins' build up an excitement which never loses sight of its purpose. Ford seems to have forgotten the meaning of the lyric in the sound of it — a strange quality in a play in which discipline and form are thematic and where emblematic material is generally under careful control.

Yet there is music of a different kind in the cold, clear and measured lines spoken by Calantha in sentencing Orgilus:

> thy confession
> Unhappy Orgilus, dooms thee a sentence ...
>
> Bloody relater of thy stains in blood,
> For that thou hast reported him, whose fortunes
> And life by thee are both at once snatched from him,
> With honourable mention, make thy choice
> Of what death likes thee best; there's all our bounty.
>
> (V.2:p.273-4)

In these few reticent lines a whole tragic experience is gathered up, but the effect of its understatement depends upon the speaker's sensitivity to the shape of the verse — the cool restraint of the opening statement, the slowing-down of the speech rhythm by the monosyllabic line 'And life by thee are both at once snatched from him', the recovery of movement at 'With honourable mention' and the unemotional withdrawal at 'there's all our bounty'. The words are matter-of-fact, it is the modulation of the verse that conveys feeling which Calantha will not permit herself to express. This is Ford at his best.

In a play where pattern, imagery and style so easily associate with music, the unusual number of opportunities for musical interludes is not surprising. It would of course be very acceptable to the audience at Blackfriars, where music was a particular attraction. Each of the three 'discovery' scenes — that of Ithocles' chamber, of Penthea's veiled body and of the altar of coronation — is introduced with a song or, in the last instance, with instrumental music. The final episode closes with another song.

All this calls for careful production, yet mechanically, considering its flexibility, the staging appears to be remarkably simple. Presumably, other than windows, there was no upper acting level at Blackfriars. *The Broken Heart* requires no upper stage, no window except that which Bassanes determines to have 'dammed up' (II.1), indicating no doubt, a window in the stage front overlooking 'a room in Bassanes' house'. A characteristic is the frequent use of the stage as a whole, often involving the entire cast. In most of these great scenes, although the opening may be formal and statuesque, there is a sense of continuous movement in and out; obviously the doors at the back and sides of the stage were in constant use.

The scene (I.2) in which Ithocles is welcomed home is the first of many in which Ford's use of the hangings and planning of stage shifting are fascinating to watch. This episode requires a throne and other furnishings; it is preceded by the opening dialogue between Crotolon and Orgilus (I.1) and concludes when the Court has left the stage, with the brief bantering between the two soldiers and their ladies. Neither passage would require more than the front stage; but the following scene (I.3), 'a grove' in the palace gardens, demands more acting space and perhaps more scenery. It opens with talk between Orgilus and Tecnicus, which can be imagined taking place in the latter's study, but after Tecnicus has left it continues with the entrance of Prophilus and Euphranea to the disguised Orgilus, presumably in the grove itself.

All this points to a carefully contrived use of cross-stage hangings — opened for the entrance of the King and the Court, closed at their exit to allow time for changing properties and scene, and perhaps not opened again until the exit of Tecnicus, after which there must be acting space for the lovers to come upon Orgilus and for the latter to play a part in which the audience share his confidence.

In this connection an episode of particular interest is the 'discovery' of Ithocles with Penthea beside him (III.2), preceded by a short passage requiring only the front stage. There is 'a song within' while several characters pass over the stage to visit Ithocles. It is with a touch of low comedy that Bassanes and Grausis, both experienced eavesdroppers, return to 'listen in different places'. We know that a curtained booth was used at Blackfriars but this somewhat clumsy piece of apparatus could not allow the space and flexibility that imaginative use of hangings can give in any theatre. It seems evident that all this preliminary business takes place in front of the closed hangings which open to disclose the brother and sister. When Bassanes followed by Grausis rudely interrupts them the actors probably move forward, so that during the subsequent noisy exchanges and the final talk between Bassanes and Grausis, when the stage is otherwise empty, the hangings can be closed again to prepare for the Court scene to welcome the Prince of Argos, which immediately follows. The 'discovery' of the dead Penthea and of the coronation altar both follow a full Court scene and both are preceded by a thinning out of characters towards the end of the previous episode.[16] Throughout the play Ford seems to have planned the use of hangings in relation to the action and the properties required for it with considerable freedom and workmanlike efficiency.

As is usual with Ford the final episode is designed to give the visual stimulus which the audience appreciated. The stage directions here are meticulous and elaborate — 'an altar covered in white, two lights of virgin wax upon it ... Ithocles on a hearse (in a rich robe with a crown on his head) .. Calantha in white crowned' — yet on examination the requirements consist of little more than small or easily movable objects. But the objects are of emblematic significance, for this is a marriage as well as a coronation, emphasised by lavish but specific costume. Equal attention is given to the musical accompaniment — recorders play for the formal entrance, cease during Calantha's devotions, after which there is 'soft music'. Even here Ford demands little of the stage itself other than efficiency and good timing; but he exacts a good deal from everyone working upon it. The classical simplicity of the apparent stage requirements in *The Broken Heart* is worth noting in a play so full of opportunities for scenic display and written for an audience to whom, for the greater part, drama meant spectacle. In its subordination of effects to speed and clarity *The Broken Heart* is a refusal to compromise.

In returning to the basic pattern of classical tragedy Ford has taken the Revenge motive, and lifted it to the level of those suprahuman forces which shape and build upon the wills and instincts of men and women. The balance of vengeance on the human level with the restoration of order from the divine viewpoint is at the heart of the *Oresteia* as of a great deal of other Greek tragedy; but since the gods are evidently using the human characters as instruments of their own purposes neither avenger nor the guilty victim can be termed just or unjust. Ford's major modification is in introducing a moral distinction between the vengeance which grows through the generations like a poison, and the retribution which hurts in order to heal. But he also shows that the Jacobean exploration of the complexities of the human mind, to which Burton had given such impetus, could be contained within the impersonal formality of Aeschylean tragedy. *The Broken Heart* is the climax of Ford's experimentation with Revenge Tragedy. This fusion of the Elizabethan tragic experience with the classical view of life, a fusion of apparent opposites, was perhaps Ford's greatest gift to the theatre of his day. For it brought to the Caroline stage a new profundity in tragedy; it also offered a fresh approach to the familiar themes of love, ambition and revenge through the medium of what was of permanent value in the theatre of the past. It also enabled him to project on the stage, both in the individual and in the group, that constancy to truth which emerges from Ford's work as the basis of healthy living.

6 Revival of Chronicle History at the Phoenix in *Perkin Warbeck*

In outline the plot of *Perkin Warbeck* begins where that of *The Broken Heart* ends. Like Nearchus Henry Tudor brings a new dynasty — 'a new soul, a new birth, in [his] sacred person' (I.1:p.384). The house of Lancaster has replaced the house of York, the tyrant Richard III is dead and the country is freed from bloodshed — but not for long. Time has already tried the new dynasty in the imposture of Lambert Simnel, now Henry's falconer, fostered in his claim to the throne as Earl of Warwick by Margaret Duchess of Burgundy, the most dangerous survivor of the house of York. Now a new pretender, again at the Duchess' instigation, threatens Henry in Perkin Warbeck, who appears as Richard Duke of York, the younger of the two sons of Edward IV, supposed murdered in the Tower. Warbeck's meteoric career, with his ability to carry and sustain his role as the rightful claimant to the throne, with his gifts of personality which enabled him to persuade of his identity the Kings of France and Scotland, the last of whom, James IV, went so far as to marry him to his first cousin Lady Katherine Gordon, is one of the unsolved riddles of history. For Ford it was evidently one of those unusual cases of human temperament and predicament which never failed to stimulate his imagination.

A return to the chronicle history play by a dramatist habitually writing for them could hardly fail to catch the interest of the audience at the Phoenix. But *Perkin Warbeck* offers more than a revival. Some major themes of *The Broken Heart* are developed or restated here; for instance the problem of the true and the false is balanced equivocally between the King who sits on the throne and the 'king' who lays claim to it, and the quest for a 'real happiness' is underlined in the durability of Katherine's love for Warbeck. But in the forefront of the play is set the typically Caroline conflict between love and honour in Lady Katherine's rejection of Dalyell's suit for the responsibilities of royal birth. Before Warbeck is even talked of

scenes, Katherine has committed herself and the
oice of priorities is kept alive later by Huntley's
lyell's undemanding loyalty. This is secondary
e situation lends a curiously enigmatic colour
to the relations between Katherine and Warbeck and thence to
the meaning of the play. Historical events are seen as the
consequence not only of the ambitions of power-seekers, but
also of the fallacious thinking of idealists. *Perkin Warbeck*
modifies both the slant of the normal historical play and the
assumptions of Caroline romance. It is a dramatic presentation of the ideals and fallibilities of kingship and, more
important, of the search for truth in a world where reality and
illusion are increasingly indistinguishable.

The play leans heavily upon Bacon's *History of the Reign of
King Henry VII* of 1623, a debt which Ford acknowledges in
the Dedication — 'a late both learned and an honourable pen'
— but there may be other sources. Some speeches are clear
transcripts from Thomas Gainsford's *The True and
Wonderful History of Perkin Warbeck* of 1618. There are
intermittent verbal echoes of both works but most of the key
images seem to derive from Bacon. A notable example is the
echo of Bacon's half-jocular identification of pretenders with
apparitions. 'At this time the King began to be haunted with
sprites by the magic and curious arts of the Lady Margaret'[1]. —
which sets up in Ford's imagination a sequence of associations
which are to be functional to the intention of the play. On the
other hand while the conception of Warbeck as smoking
straw — 'this smoke of straw' (I.1:p.387) — may be suggested
by Bacon's comment that Warbeck was 'smoked away from
France', it probably owes something to Gainsford's
association of Warbeck with both smoke and straw — for he
was 'an Idol, a Puppet as it were, made of straw and painted
cloth' and 'all these were but smoking illusions'.[2]

Considering the care with which Ford follows Bacon's
account of events, however, his departure from it is significant.
When at Henry's instigation, Hialus the Spanish agent visits
James of Scotland to make overtures of peace, a move which is
only later followed up with a proposal of marriage with
Henry's daughter, Ford telescopes events so that the marriage
proposal coincides with negotiations for peace. Thus James'
motives for dismissing Warbeck are coloured by a political

expediency which compares with Henry's own simultaneous negotiations for a Spanish match for his heir Prince Arthur — a suitable double foil to Warbeck's sole request of his quondam supporter not to deprive him of the beloved wife he has bestowed upon him. Again according to Bacon — and to historical tradition — Warbeck confesses to imposture before his death. In the play he never wavers from the conviction that he is indeed the rightful King of England, and Bacon's comment that 'with long and continued counterfeiting' he 'was turned by habit almost into the thing he seemed to be'[3] is echoed in the play by Henry Tudor — 'the custom sure of being styled a king Hath fastened in his thought that he is such' (V.2:p.461) — a biased judgement! Henry may be right — history assures us that he was — but in the slant of the play the verdict is ambiguous. Although, apart from these deliberate reshapings of fact, Ford's treatment of places and events is scrupulously accurate, the story of Perkin Warbeck remains a 'mystery'.

A feature of the play is the characters' obsession with time. Time and fate are frequently associated as when Frion, Warbeck's hard-worked Secretary, reassures himself by linking time and fate with a full tide carrying his faction forward:

> Flow to a full sea; time alone debates
> Quarrels fore-written in the book of fates.
>
> (II.3:p.416)

Later Warbeck makes time the agent of their fate:

> time and industry
> Will show us better days and end the worst.
>
> (IV.3:p.447)

And Henry sees time as the restorer of order:

> Time may restore their wits whom vain ambition
> Hath many years distracted.
>
> (V.2:p.461)

Both Warbeck and Lady Katherine are conscious of time as arbiter; they have been 'spectacles to time and pity' (V.1:p.454);

but time can be cheated — 'impoverish time of its amazement,
friends' is Warbeck's encouragement to his followers as he and
they face death, but as he goes to execution Stanley sees time's
irony turned against himself when it becomes the instrument
of fate:

>   fate and time
> Have wheeled about to turn me into nothing.
>
> (II.2:p.407)

Throughout the action there is a constant preoccupation with
the swift passage of time, the need to use time well, the
importance of being 'on time'. 'Our time requires dispatch ...
we trifle time ... here to linger More time is but to lose it ... Our
time of stay doth seem too long.' The total impression is of
time passing like a perpetually moving backcloth. The
characters must keep up with it, seize the moment before it
passes or lose their role. It is an accompaniment to the action
which keeps in mind the inexorable march of events within
which the characters can shape their destinies only to a limited
extent.

Against this background Ford's balancing of events in
England and in Scotland is masterly. The play opens in
Henry's presence chamber, but with a sense of uneasiness:

> Still to be haunted, still to be pursued,
> Still to be frighted with false apparitions
> Of pageant majesty and new-coined greatness,
> As if we were a mockery king in state.

The lines recall the opening of Shakespeare's *Henry IV, Part I*:

> So shaken as we are, so wan with care
> Find we a time for frighted peace to pant.

It is clear that Henry Tudor, like Henry Bolingbroke, knows
his hold upon the throne is tenuous. It is with the same
uneasiness that at the end of this expository scene, Henry
decides, on receiving a letter of which the contents are not
revealed, to move his Court to the Tower. But the following
scene transports us to the as yet untroubled Court of Scotland
where, in an important little episode, Dalyell presents his suit

to the Earl of Huntley for the hand of his daughter. When Katherine enters, her apprehension of royal status, her determination not to let her heart obscure her judgement, are expressed with a verbal involvement which has a ring of false conviction; the impression is deepened by Huntley's discomfort and Dalyell's chivalrous acceptance of a situation at variance with his simplicity of nature. It is characteristic of Ford — a characteristic which his theatre seems to have countenanced by now — to place the two sides of the question fairly before the audience, and it is in this context that we are to see the reception of Warbeck by the Scottish King and his Court. When the action swings back again to England and the defection of some of Henry's most trusted friends, the discovery and sentencing of Stanley and the shame of Clifford the informer are an effective foil to Warbeck's triumph in Scotland. Katherine who now believes she is ruled both by her heart and by her head, readily accepts marriage with Warbeck; the Scottish king has now recognised and instated him as a kinsman and brother prince and all is ready for the march into England; only the old and over-cautious — Huntley and Crawford — are doubtful. And now, not until this climax of his success, does Ford introduce Warbeck's followers.

Frion's task in humouring 'this abject scum of mankind' is the first shadow to be cast upon Warbeck's hopes. Bacon has no record of Skelton, Astley, Heron and the Mayor of Cork until Warbeck's second attempt in Ireland after his dismissal from Scotland. Ford's anticipation of their appearance, and just at this moment, is deliberate. It is often objected that *Perkin Warbeck* is no history play. In fact Ford seems to rewrite history; for up to this point the emphasis upon Henry's troubles in England — contrasted visibly on stage with Warbeck's conquest of a reigning king and his Court, not by force but by the kingliness of his person and behaviour, and his more important conquest of a royal princess, combined with his own conviction that he is what he claims to be — challenges the historical viewpoint. Would not a playgoer ignorant of history take Warbeck at this juncture to be the rightful king? Ironically it is here, at this first climax of the play, that the possibility that Warbeck's fortunes may desert him is thrust upon us by the first appearance of his unlikely entourage. Meantime in another English episode we find

Henry with the confidence and expertise of a soldier king,
arming his forces first to quell the rising in Cornwall and then
to march north where at Norham Castle Bishop Fox plants in
Scottish minds serious doubts as to Warbeck's claim. The
arrival of the Spanish agent Hialus, whom we meet in
subsequent scenes, first in England, then in Scotland, brings
the English and the Scottish Courts together and the action
begins to link the two sides of the plot.

Henry is now in the ascendant, but the same balanced
treatment continues. As Henry has been deceived where he
trusted most, so is Warbeck, for as Stanley deserts Henry, so
James IV deserts Warbeck. As Henry grieves for his subjects'
blood after the suppression of the Cornish rising (III.1:p.420),
so Warbeck grieves for the spoiling of the countryside after the
discomfiture at Norham Castle (III.4:p.433). By this delicate
poise of the rivals in balancing circumstances Ford builds up
an ironic comment not only upon Warbeck's pretentions but
also on Henry's own status. What after all, is there to choose
between these two contenders? Which is the true king and
which the false? Is Henry after all, in some deeper sense than
any that history can record, 'a mockery king in show'?[4]

The irony is driven home by Ford's development of the idea
of witchcraft. The theme is built upon a hint in Bacon, already
quoted, which reappears in the first lines of the play — that
the king began to be 'haunted' by the arts of the Lady Margaret
who 'raised up the ghost of Richard Duke of York to walk and
vex the King' (Bacon, p.386). Henry refers to the two
pretenders, Lambert Simnel and Perkin Warbeck, as 'false
apparitions' and the accusation of illusion by sorcery is
constantly levelled at Warbeck by his enemies. No sooner is the
marriage with Katherine celebrated than Huntley refers to the
pair as 'King Oberon and Queen Mab' and meantime Henry is
negotiating with Hialus in what he describes as 'a charm in
secret that shall unloose The witchcraft wherewith young
James is bound' (III.1:p.418). Later the same argument is used
to convince King James that he has been mistaken in Warbeck
— 'a silly creature ... As is but in effect an apparition, A
shadow, a mere trifle' (IV.3:p.441). Reference to witchcraft
crowd up in the last scene on Tower Hill where Urswick
identifies Warbeck himself with the witch — 'inveighing to
thy party with thy witchcraft Young Edward Earl of Warwick';

and later, shocked by Warbeck's unshakeable confidence, he
says:

> Thus witches
> Possessed, even to their deaths deluded, say
> They have been wolves and dogs and sailed in egg-shells ...
>
> the enemy of mankind
> Is powerful, but false, and falsehood confident.
>
> (V.3:p.467)

The assumption is that just as a witch, having been used by the
devil, is abandoned in disillusionment, so Warbeck is now
abandoned and left to his fate. Scene by scene the idea of
forbidden arts confusing fact with appearance, reality with
dream, is built round Warbeck. Even his closest supporters
begin to have their doubts: King James at Norham — 'Duke of
York, for such thou sayst thou art', Frion in a private
consultation following the undermining of his status by the
visit of Hialus to the Scottish Court — 'if you will appear a
prince indeed'. The whole situation at the end of the play is
ponderously summarised by the Mayor of Cork — 'kings must
be kings and subjects subjects, but which is which you shall
pardon me for that' (V.2:p.461); and when the rebellion is over
Henry dismisses the whole matter as 'some unquiet dream'
(V.2:p.457)).

It is in his reactions to the constant flux between the real and
the unreal and between good and evil fortune that Warbeck
ceases to be the historical figure of Bacon's or Gainsford's
account, for his whole career in the play provides a comment
upon the two reigning kings as theirs does upon him. The two
sides of the action are mutually illuminating and often
sharply contrasting. While Henry Tudor is uneasy from the
first words he speaks, there is never any doubt in Warbeck's
mind as to the justice of his cause nor does his faith in himself
ever waver. Considering his supposed brother's murder and
the threat to his own life in infancy, and the privations he has
suffered in manhood, Warbeck would have ample excuse in
moments of success for the brash sarcasm which Henry
permits himself — 'Trim Duke Perkin ... This cub ... this
gewgaw ... this smoke of straw ... this meteor ... this airy

apparition.' When Warbeck's hopes in Scotland are lost,
Henry indulges his triumph in ironic visions of a counterfeit
king — 'Must Perkin wear the crown? ... King Perkin will in
progress ride ... let us meet him and tender homage' (IV.4).
True this piece of *hubris* is matched by Astley's exclamation
after a temporary success in Cornwall — 'All's cock sure'
(IV.5:p.452), but Warbeck himself never endorses it and the
parallel is no credit to the King of England! Not that Warbeck
is without his moments of exhilaration, but when he gives
voice to his assured hopes it is on an idealistic level. As he
leaves Katherine after his initial success in Scotland he assures
her of a more than political outcome:

> my business
> Attends on fortune of a sprightlier triumph;
> For love and majesty are reconciled,
> And vow to crown thee empress of the west.
>
> (III.2:p.427)

He is inspired, not dazzled by their greatness. Warbeck is a
dreamer and the lesson of fact is something he has yet to learn,
but there is nothing of petty advantage or personal ambition
in his dreams.

A comparison between Henry's reaction to bad faith in
Stanley and Warbeck's dignified and fair-minded reception of
King James' excuses for abandoning him, again places the
royalty of nature on Warbeck's side. Warbeck knows where
gratitude is due and like a king, he gives it. Warbeck realises
that this is the beginning of the end yet he makes of it another
occasion for reminding himself and his hearers of his identity:

> Witness Edward's blood in me! I am
> More loth to part with such a great example
> Of virtue than all other mere respects.
>
> (IV.3:p.444)

In contrast Henry's reaction is a breakdown into threats and
self-pity which draws from Durham the rebuke — 'you lose
your constant temper'. Only once in the entire play does
Warbeck lose confidence; this is in the short scene with Frion
after the advent of Hialus, but even here he can disarm Frion's

discontent, first by a personal appeal — 'I prithee be not angry' — and then by his renewed determination — 'if my cousin-king will fail Our cause will never' (IV.2:p.439).

The impression we have of Henry is of a king who can be both ruthless and gentle, coolly efficient in war but with the wisdom to value negotiation higher than force — in fact the historical figure of Henry VII. But underneath all this the play stresses the inescapable insecurity of the usurper. To Warbeck Henry is 'cunning in his plots' and his instrument is the 'fox', the wily Bishop Fox of Durham. Warbeck has no cunning plots to aid his cause, only his faith in the invulnerability of truth and the compelling force of his sense of his own royalty — qualities which have earned him the entrée to the Courts of princes, above all the fateful visit to King James' Court in Scotland.

Characteristically Ford leaves us to draw our own conclusions as to King James' motives. We overhear no confidential discussion, all we know is that the more experienced members of his Court are not with him in his wholesale acceptance of the claimant. The situation is pointed up by the hostile attitude of so honest a man as Huntley, Katherine's father:

> Let me be a dotard,
> A bedlam, a poor sot, or what you please
> To have me, so you will not stain your blood,
> Your own blood royal, sir, though mixed with mine,
> By marriage of this girl to a straggler.
>
> (II.3:p.411)

James' reply is worthy of Richard II reacting to the warnings of the dying John of Gaunt:

> Kings are counterfeits
> In your repute, grave oracle, not presently
> Set on their thrones with sceptres in their fists.
> But use your own detraction; tis our pleasure
> To give our cousin York for wife our kinswoman.

James' wilfulness and imperious irresponsibility contrast sharply with Katherine's grave scruples and Warbeck's restrained triumph.

But James is a realist even in self-will and when the Scottish army with Warbeck's scanty following is drawn up under the walls of Norham Castle, both leaders face the hard fact of circumstance which throws them into startling relief. For James kings can make mistakes and a wise king knows how to get out of trouble. Loyalty, friendship, pity are luxuries no commander can afford when he finds himself on the losing side. For the kingly virtues of mercy and of concern for a 'people afflicted' and a 'land depopulated' which we have already seen in Henry and which Warbeck voices now, he has nothing but contempt — why be 'Ridiculously careful of an interest Another man possesseth?' — and Warbeck's higher thoughts are cut short with the practical question — 'Where's your faction?' James has supported Warbeck only so long as he seems to be a good investment, but nothing could more clearly demonstrate the sheer ineptitude, in James' world, of Warbeck's sense of integrity which the shrewd Scottish lords dismiss as 'effeminately dolent'. Plainly the sphere of power politics in which the two kings move is one in which Warbeck can never be at home.

The meeting between Henry and Warbeck is a departure from historical record which Ford evidently found essential to his theme. For Warbeck, in whom the worst of failure has only steeled his faith in 'the divinity of royal birth', the encounter is of true Prince with reigning Prince. Subtly, so far, the impression has been established that Warbeck is the better man, but the issue is not so simple. Warbeck stands silent while the King gazes at him, and remarks that he sees 'no wonder', only 'an ornament of nature'. Henry's charges of pride, of youthful irresponsibility Warbeck dismisses with a quiet affirmation of his rightful status as he reminds Henry of his own tortuous advancement to power:

There was a shooting in of light when Richmond
Not aiming at a crown, retired and gladly
For comfort to the Duke of Bretaine's court.

(V.2:p.459)

Bosworth field was 'A morn to Richmond and a night to Richard', but the hard-won triumph might as easily have been a failure like his own.

Unmoved by the indignation of the English lords Henry
stands fascinated, encouraging rather than rebuking the sheer
audacity that faces him. His scornful rejoinder that what
Warbeck 'learnt by heart' from his 'Duchess aunt' is 'now
received for truth' and his later comment that 'The custom
sure of being styled a king Hath fashioned in his thought that
he is one' may be an acceptable psychological solution,[5] but
Warbeck himself demonstrates its total irrelevance. Scorn he
says, is fashioned to appeal to 'gazers' eyes' but 'Truth in her
pure simplicity wants art To put a feigned blush on'; and he
proceeds to disappoint the onlookers by merely pleading like a
king, for his unfortunate followers. What Henry encounters
here is a new kind of truth — not truth as he and his world
know it, measured by good sense and expediency, but truth to a
man's own self and his conviction of what that self should be.

The episode gives a good deal of opportunity to the actor who
plays Henry Tudor. The significance of the dialogue is in
Henry's readiness to listen — if, on the one hand, this is 'antic
pageantry'. nowhere else does Henry give such attention to a
traitor under arrest. The whole set of this small interlude
suggests that Warbeck and Henry are complementary; each has
what the other lacks of kingship. We have seen Henry's unease
contrasted with Warbeck's confidence, Henry's restlessness
contrasted with Warbeck's serenity, Henry's chicanery
contrasted with Warbeck's simplicity — above all Warbeck's
personal life, though distanced for reasons which are discussed
below, contrasted with Henry's apparent lack of it. We have
also seen Warbeck's lack of practical expertise contrasted with
Henry's mastery of circumstance, Warbeck's failure to use his
advantage contrasted with Henry's opportunism. Step by
step, in the skilful alternation of scenes from both sides of the
plot, the two rivals have been drawing together. Time and
events have marked Henry as the successful ruler and Warbeck
as the counterfeit, but when they meet in a sort of mutual
respect as man to man, the episode invites us to reverse the
verdict.

The final scene on Tower Hill resolves the problem of the
play. Warbeck has been sentenced to death but he must first be
humiliated in the stocks before a jeering populace. Now
stripped of everything of material value, Warbeck faces the
final test of his integrity in the taunts of Lambert Simnel, like

himself a failed pretender, but one who has managed to survive.

Lambert Simnel's advice to listen to Urswick's counsel and confess is not altogether unkind. This is what he has done and has he not done pretty well? He has comfort and security, above all he has escaped 'the hangman's clutches'. 'Be no longer a counterfeit', he urges, 'confess and hope for pardon' (V.3:p.465). Warbeck has already drawn a clear distinction between princes and ordinary men — 'Subjects are men on earth, kings men and gods' (IV.5:p.452). This is the conviction that has carried him so far and that will arm him now. To Warbeck who has suffered in mind for those who have died in his cause, Simnel represents all that he has hoped to destroy. The baseness of Simnel's origin, the falseness of a cause which, like his own, cost lives, is proved by his reaction to defeat. Here is a man who has failed in constancy; never true at heart he has never known integrity — 'coarse creatures are incapable of excellence' (V.3:p.465). Warbeck has outfaced Henry Tudor with the simplicity of truth as he sees it, he now confronts Lambert Simnel with all that he has left for posterity — 'a martyrdom of majesty'. Again a further step in degradation in the world's eyes sharpens Warbeck's apprehension of what a king should be. Together the two confrontations define the intention of the play. Henry could find no answer to Warbeck's challenge; to Lambert Simnel. Warbeck is simply mad.

Lady Katherine's entrance is well placed at this point. For the last time, in a passage quoted above, the pretender's claim is identified with the illusions of witchcraft: 'Thus witches Possessed, even to their deaths deluded' — Urswick's words give the concept an almost visual prominence. But Katherine finally scatters it by applying to it her own clear statement of what she knows is real:

> When the holy churchman joined our hands
> Our vows were real then; the ceremony
> Was not an apparition but in act.

> (V.3:p.467)

Her defence — a brave one in the face of incredulous noblemen and a hostile crowd — 'I am certain thou art my husband' carries Warbeck over the final step to his real kingship:

Even when I fell I stood enthroned a monarch
Of one chaste wife's troth pure and uncorrupted.

Like Ithocles trapped and defeated by Orgilus, Warbeck's integrity has earned its own crown and he can say of his rival, 'A woman's faith hath robbed thy fame of triumph.' It is with this confidence that he leaves his friends dispensing parting favours in his wishes — all he has — like a king.

For Ford the fascination of the controversial history of Perkin Warbeck was less the difference between the false and the true than the difference between two kinds of truth. A reigning king must follow wisdom as the world recognises it, but there is a better kind of wisdom in a man's truth to himself through the trials of time and circumstances. This is the real kingliness of nature which we see Henry striving for at every crisis in his fortunes, but which Warbeck possesses already in himself. The issue between Henry and Warbeck is complicated in that each is justified in his own sphere of life, but the two worlds never link for there is always a King James of Scotland or a Lambert Simnel in the way. In this issue Lady Katherine functions as a mean.

Surprisingly Professor Alfred Harbage fastens upon the Lady Katherine, Huntley and Dalyell scenes in particular as evidence for Dekker's part-authorship of the play.[6] No doubt Ford was influenced by Dekker — which of the contemporary dramatists was not? We know that he collaborated with Dekker earlier in *The Witch of Edmonton*, and it would be natural that something of Dekker's humanity and expertise should rub off on his own work. But Harbage's comparison of Katherine and Huntley with Bellafront and Friscobaldo in Dekker's *The Honest Whore* II points only to Ford's skill in making of a hint from another source something new and peculiarly his own. Huntley has Friscobaldo's blunt forthrightness (but so for that matter has Bassanes in *The Broken Heart*), he has also his fatherly concern for a misguided daughter whose marriage choice he cannot approve, a concern which Dalyell does not allow us to forget when the action moves away from him. But Huntley is in a very different category from Dekker's testy old men. Brief as is the space he occupies in the action Huntley is a tragic figure as Friscobaldo is not. In Huntley there is from the outset a conflict between what is due from the father of a royal princess and the natural instinct which would prompt him to encourage Dalyell's suit for her hand. Throughout the scene of his first appearance (I.2), Huntley strives to convince his judgement against his heart. There is no such complexity in Friscobaldo nor do we see Dekker's characters, as a rule, in the false position which Huntley has to sustain in the Scottish Court as events carry Katherine towards what is to him a disastrous mistake. Again there is no parallel in Friscobaldo, ruthless as he can be, with the bitterness that inspires Huntley's sardonic comments on the wedding celebrations and, later, his counsel that Katherine must forget her title 'to old Huntley's family' if she will have peace, a valediction which Katherine calls 'the cruellest farewell' (IV.3:p.446). Nor even in the final scene does Huntley withdraw from his position; like many characters in Ford's plays, Huntley can be detached even in pity. His last words to the lovers give not a syllable to feeling and when both have left the stage, Katherine to vowed widowhood and Warbeck to execution, he has nothing left to say:

> I have
> Not thoughts left; 'tis sufficient in such cases
> Just laws ought to proceed.

> (V.3:p.470)

These exit lines are clearly by Ford and it is difficult to believe that Dekker could have conceived the character whom they so aptly dismiss.

Professor Harbage sees Katherine as rather a Bellafront than a Calantha — a model of fidelity and wifely duty. This seems to me a misreading both of Lady Katherine and òf Calantha. Like Calantha Katherine embodies the very principle of royalty. As she stands in the first Huntley scene, to which we cannot turn too often to savour the irony of the play, between Huntley with his claims upon her duty as a princess of the blood and Dalyell with his offer of a sincere love, she lifts the whole concept of royalty, as Calantha lifts it, as much above the human qualities of love and pity as above material ambition and power politics. The pledge she makes to her father is of an absolute self-devotion to an ideal vocation in which, as Warbeck is to discover, the prince is both human and more than human. What she permits herself to feel for Dalyell is neither love nor pity, but compassion and the loyalty of a tried friend.

There is something designedly chilling about Katherine in this scene. Attention has already been drawn to the ambiguity suggested here in her attitude to Dalyell and its subsequent colouring of her relationship with her husband. But as with that between Ithocles and Calantha, Ford will not please his audience by allowing the love interest to overbalance the intention of the play. This is not a study of the world well lost, it is the story of a quest. But after this introductory episode Ford can release the woman from the image in a few brief passages handled with characteristic reticence and restraint. The first is the moment when Katherine, having heard Warbeck's speech before the King and Court, is overcome with emotion. This is love at first sight no doubt, but it should not be confused with the love she might have given to Dalyell. 'His words have touched me home' — his words, not his character, although we are told of his graceful bearing — and Warbeck's words concern a displaced and abused royalty. For Katherine it is 'As if his cause were mine' — plainly the feeling she expresses is in part a realisation of her pledge to her father. Fidelity and wifely duty are only subsidiary to that which carries her forward to her destiny. Katherine is entirely with Warbeck in his quest for kingship; it is this shared task, not primarily their love, that binds her to him and gives her the vision and constancy to transmute failure into a different kind of success.

Katherine has the gift of foresight, denied to Warbeck but strong enough in her to counsel and arm him against possible disaster. When the wedded couple are left alone Katherine has some lines designed to counter Warbeck's dreams of triumph, in which she seems to face, though she never puts it into words, the possibility first that he may fail, secondly that he may be mistaken. Warbeck is always serenely unaware of time's erosions but Katherine knows that 'Events of time may shorten my deserts in others' pity' (III.2:p.427), but if this happens he still has his monarchy in her. The episode is heavy with prognostication; it is also charged with that sense of time and its mutability, time and its severing referred to earlier in this chapter — even the close is ominous in its simplicity: 'Some few minutes Remain yet'. But Warbeck's reaction is in one of his few scornful references to Henry — as 'the counterfeit', an expression which Katherine instantly rebukes: 'Pray do not use That word: it carries fate in't.' If Warbeck is the dreamer, Katherine is the realist. Again we have a typical ambiguity in this remarkable little scene. Does Katherine from this point onwards begin to doubt Warbeck's claim as well as his hopes of success? If so it is his cause that she doubts, not himself, and like Calantha for her subjects she knows how to provide comfort for him if the worst should happen.

It is not until the episode on St Michael's Mount, where Katherine with Dalyell and her two servants is pursued by the Earl of Oxford, that Ford allows us to see the character in the round. The timing is excellent; when the collapse of Warbeck's cause necessitates a new dramatic interest there is revealed at last the exploited individual beneath the royal lady. The incident, the more moving for its delayed impact, suggests a new comment on the preceding historical events. So far Katherine has confronted misfortune with stoical acceptance, but when in the face of desertion, 'contempt and poverty', Jane begs her to return to Scotland, she gives vent to the pent-up feeling of one who will not scruple to name things as they are:

> the king who gave me
> Hath sent me with my husband from his presence
> Delivered me suspected to his nation,
> Rendered us spectacles to time and pity.

>   (V.1:p.454)

This is the first overt criticism of James' behaviour that we have heard; the impact is the greater when with the same royal indignation, too large for resentment, Katherine continues to assess the loyalty of her quondam friends in Scotland:

> is it fit I should return to such
> As only listen after our descent
> From happiness enjoyed to misery
> Expected though uncertain? Never, never. ...

This is the woman speaking through the princess; plainly her father's attitude has bitten deep, yet her own is something more than personal. Alone of all the princes in the play Katherine can temper ambition with judgement. Her reaction to the ultimate disaster places Henry's scheming, James' opportunism, above all Warbeck's day-dreaming, at their proper level. It is in this realistic spirit that she joins Warbeck on Tower Hill, not in defiance of their enemies but simply because her place is at her hsusband's side. Her action, her firm refusal to withdraw, turns the outraged sense of propriety in the English noblemen into a kind of pettiness — not without a touch of Ford's characteristically delicate irony.

This balancing of the real and ideal consequences of royalty in a figure conceived as half symbol, half character, was not easy and Ford could hardly have attempted it before the writing of *The Broken Heart*. As it is the two aspects of the character never entirely harmonise. The difference between Ford's handling of Calantha and Katherine is that between a deliberate distancing and a holding at arm's length. Nevertheless the reticent and gradual unfolding of a central but passive character is a useful device for implying, without overtly resolving, a moral complication at the heart of the play.[7]

A characteristic of this play is the selection of brief passages for special development, small cameos in which the drama springs into a new dimension of life. Henry's reception of the news of Stanley's treason is an outstanding example. Such passages were probably played near the front of the stage giving the impression of a close relationship with the audience — the nearest Ford comes in this play to soliloquy in depth. It is a shift of tone particularly suited to the intimacy of the Phoenix theatre; at these moments not only the main figures come to a new vitality, but less important, even background characters step into prominence. We remember Henry's barely controlled grief, but we do not easily forget the informer Clifford, a secondary figure until this episode — Clifford, his cheek wet with the cross with which Stanley signs it, Clifford struggling with shame and the false position in which his belated loyalty and mixed motives have placed him. Dramatically, for the moment Clifford becomes a more important figure than Stanley, yet the effect — one which calls for discernment as well as compassion in the dramatist — is entirely objective.

Another example is the brief dialogue in which Surrey parries King James' challenge to single combat, with the town of Berwick as ransome should the English general fail —

> the English general returns
> A sensible devotion from his heart,
> His very soul to this unfellowed grace —
>
> (IV.1:p.436)

after which he proceeds to protect himself by pointing out that Berwick is not his to give although his life he dares 'freely hazard'. Brief as it is, this interlude both illuminates the tactical skill of an otherwise background character and pinpoints a difficult and dangerous political situation. A third instance is the dialogue between Huntley and Dalyell already commented upon in another connection, which in setting out a problem of political importance — the marriage of a princess — in purely human terms, develops a new dramatic interest in the affairs of the Scottish Court. It is worth noting that all the instances referred to appear to be Ford's invention.

So also, in all but the bare fact of their existence which he had from Bacon, is the group of ill-educated followers who constitute Warbeck's entourage in Scotland. As representatives of the common man in an army on active service, Astley the scrivener, Skelton the tailor, Heron the mercer and John-a-Water, the Mayor of Cork, might have provided the welcome human touch we have in Pistol and Fluellen in *Henry IV, Part II*. As it is, Ford's delight in the extreme case prompts him to present Warbeck's closest counsellors in the shape of these peasants — presumably in order to maintain our awareness of the fragility of his expectations. Thus what might have been a sequence of significant comedy degenerates into low farce. It is perhaps one of the worst examples of Ford's limited capacity in plays after *The Broken Heart* to manage a comic sub-plot.

The play's emphasis upon the outward shows of royalty gives ample opportunity for ceremonial entrances, for colour and pageantry. Many of these entrances are accompanied by a 'flourish'. But in fact *Perkin Warbeck* is exceptionally static;

physical action is at the minimum and the greater part of the
business is carried on by discussion or debate for which, from
what can be surmised of its shape and construction, the
Phoenix theatre seems to have been well suited. There are no
battle scenes, nor do we hear from a single common soldier. It
is worth noting that several of these discussion or study scenes
are staged in semi-darkness with dim lights. For instance the
scene in the Tower (I.3) in which Henry hears of Stanley's
defection is played by candlelight and on hearing the news
Henry asks Urswick for 'the light'. No doubt the dramatic
effect depended a good deal upon this candlelight. Similarly,
the one scene in which we have Katherine and Warbeck alone
together (III.3) Jane is bidden 'set the lights down' before
leaving them. The effect would be to concentrate attention on
the lovers and the destiny they face.

An upper stage level is required on two occasions only but
both are important. These are for Lady Katherine to witness
and react to Warbeck's arrival in Court (II.1), and for the
parley at Norham Castle (III.4). It is possible that, for the first
time in Ford's independent plays, a movable booth was used
for both episodes and if painted cloth or canvas replaced the
surrounding curtains in the castle scene, the booth could be
part of a permanent set. No doubt the alteration of scenes in
the English and Scottish Courts was effected by the use of
different doors at the back and sides of the stage.

What prompted Ford to revive the chronicle history play?
After the wider horizons of *The Broken Heart* the pageant of
history as a background to human endeavour was a natural
next step. It also gave him an opportunity for a last word on yet
another well-tried Elizabethan dramatic form before turning
his attention to domestic drama. But *Perkin Warbeck* is more
than a chronicle history as such. Ford's historical sense is un-
questioned especially in the English scenes, and if he
rearranges events he never falsifies them. But Professor Anderson's suggestion that the play may have been prompted by
Ford's interest in 'the privileges and responsibilities of sovereignty' seems to me an interesting half-explanation.[8] The play
is typically Caroline. It projects an essentially aristocratic view
of history in which the common people have no place even as
background to the princes and power-seekers who make
history. Its concern is with individuals of finer grain than their

fellows, heroic in their aspirations and in what they believe of
themselves, vainly trying to match their strength against the
relentless course of time. It is a record of attitudes rather than
of actions and of the tensions between motives and circumstances. In this sense *Perkin Warbeck* is both a natural sequel
to *The Broken Heart* and a first step towards the heroic tragedy
of the Restoration theatre.

But the quest for the kingly man, the search for the truth
which is the first requirement of the kingly mind, is a matter
for moral allegory. In trying to contain such an allegory
within a historical plot Ford was undertaking a difficult task.
Particularly in the Scottish scenes there is from time to time a
certain uneasiness, a loosening of artistic purpose. Yet
perhaps no one has given a more convincing picture of Henry
Tudor or of the fascinating and elusive figure of Perkin
Warbeck. Few plays could be better calculated to suggest a
rethinking of history or to leave in the mind such compelling
unanswered questions. It is strange that the play has received
so little attention in this century, for it offers both to the
director and to the individual actor a breadth of interpretation
seldom found in Elizabethan historical drama but more
familiar in our time. We should be grateful to Ford that after
this thoughtful presentation of a controversial subject Perkin
Warbeck remains in his hands an enigma.

7 Return to Domestic Tragi-comedy at the Phoenix: *The Lady's Trial* and *The Fancies Chaste and Noble*

In *Perkin Warbeck* Ford had completed his experiment with tragedy. Between *The Lover's Melancholy* and that play he had explored from one angle after another the problem of preserving the integrity of the individual against the pressures of established moral and social codes, against the tensions of pride, ambition, lust and love, and against the inexorable march of human events. Now he was to turn to the predicament of the individual confronted with the claims and prejudices of a sophisticated society. Considering the current taste in the private theatre to which Jonson responded in his Caroline plays, this theme could have formed the basis of social satire. But Ford approached the subject as a human problem; he needed a fresh pattern and he looked for his model in the domestic drama of the early years of the Century.

In the two plays considered here, and especially in *The Lady's Trial*, Ford was in fact turning back. He had worked with Dekker in domestic tragedy in *The Witch of Edmonton* and the influence of Dekker is often to be found in his handling of women characters. For instance the conception of Levidolche in *The Lady's Trial*, her struggle for poise and reinstatement, may owe something to Dekker's Bellafront in *The Honest Whore*. Flavia, in the sub-plot of *The Fancies*, is a reflection of Winnifred, probably mainly his own contribution, in *The Witch of Edmonton*; both women are deceived and exploited by their husbands, both remain faithful in affection and there is some similarity in behaviour. But Ford's familiarity with Heywood's two domestic tragedies, *A Woman Killed With Kindness* of about 1603 and *The English Traveller*, printed in 1633 but acted some years earlier,[1] is undeniable and it seems to have had a lasting impact upon his work.

Attention has already been drawn to the close-knit family atmosphere even of Ford's Princes' Courts, especially in *The*

Broken Heart and *The Lover's Melancholy*, and the affinity between *Love's Sacrifice* and *The English Traveller* has been noted.[2] Always behind Ford's mind is the attraction of the domestic triangle — wife, husband, husband's friend — and the fallibility of the friend who may abuse or exploit the trust reposed in him. The importance to lovers of friendship and its possible dangers are stated in *The Lover's Melancholy*, developed in *Love's Sacrifice* and become a major theme in *The Lady's Trial*. Verbal echoes are few but there is some indication that Ford knew Heywood's work well enough to reassess the two domestic tragedies so that he could impose upon the sententiousness of *A Woman Killed with Kindness* a new theme, perhaps suggested from *The English Traveller*, of the damage the innocent may sustain not only in fact, but also in reputation when they fall into the hands of either the unscrupulous or the misguided.

THE FANCIES CHASTE AND NOBLE, A PLAY WITH A CHANGED INTENTION?

The relevance to this chapter of *The Fancies Chaste and Noble* lies primarily in the domestic interest of its sub-plot, but the play as a whole is worth considering for the use Ford makes of so unlikely a secondary theme in a drama which has many elements of the typical tragedy of revenge, and in particular of *The Revenger's Tragedy*. As I shall try to show, the play has a further interest in a possible change of intention.

As the play stands the contradiction between the dénouement and what we are led to expect in the first three acts has been taken as evidence of Ford's desire to trick or surprise his audience. But in fact, apart from this play, Ford is careful to build up an expectation of what is to happen; surprise is generally within an episode to quicken interest or point the action — as for instance Calantha's reaction to ill news, Hippolita drinking her own poison, Vasques' sudden reversal from sympathy to overt cruelty in his treatment of Putana, Auria's change from rebuke to praise in the final scene of *The Lady's Trial*. In thus tricking the audience with a reversal of all that has gone before *The Fancies* would appear to be unique.[3] On the other hand the play is a good example of

Ford's own development upon the earlier domestic drama in exposing the petty intrigues and morally compromising situations in which people involve themselves in pursuit of relationships.

The main action of *The Fancies* turns upon Octavio, Marquis of Sienna, who keeps in his Court three unidentified young women known as the Fancies — apparently for his pleasure though later we learn that he is supposed to be impotent. The plot is sparked off in the first scene when Troylo-Savelli, nephew to Octavio, persuades his friend Livio to seek advancement for himself and his sister Castamela by introducing her to the Court, where she will join the Fancies. At first hesitant, brother and sister eventually agree to the proposal and Castamela makes a break to her lover Romanello on the grounds that since neither of them is rich, she will not stand in the way of his fortunes. Romanello however follows Castamela to Court disguised as a malcontent. Meantime, believing that the Fancies are Octavio's harem, Castamela is at first as reluctant as Romanello is critical; then her attitude changes to one of serenity in which, to the surprise and perturbation of her brother Livio, she determines to remain at Court.

Now this scene (IV.1) seems to be the significant turning-point in the play. Up to this point Castamela and Troylo have little contact and do not appear to share any affection. Yet in the final act we are asked to accept that Troylo loves Castamela and has lured her with her brother to Court hoping that Romanello will believe her corrupt and reject her so that he, Troylo, can marry her himself; moreover we learn that, far from being a sensualist, Octavio is a kind uncle, for the Fancies are his orphaned nieces whom he has taken into his care.

This curious resolution is perhaps best measured against the sub-plot concerning Flavia, Romanello's sister. When Flavia's husband Fabricio deserts her and for gain, repudiates her in open court on the grounds of a precontract, Romanello characteristically believes her to be the guilty party. In fact the reverse is the truth and when married, apparently happily, to the Lord Julio, Flavia neither forgets her love for her first husband nor neglects in her new prosperity to help him in his need. Flavia is the loyal wife, a conception no doubt derived from *The Honest Whore*, and she emerges from treachery and slander with her nature unimpaired. If Ford was following his usual habit of making the sub-plot, however disconnected circumstantially, underline the main plot, it would be reasonable to expect the heroine of the main story to pass through not imaginary, but real moral dangers; moreover the presence of Romanello as a malcontent in a supposedly corrupt Court might recall that of Vindice in the Ducal Court in *The Revenger's Tragedy*, thus pointing to a very different development in the last two acts.

In fact the impression of absolute corruption in Octavio's Court is built up with meticulous care. In the opening scene Troylo's attempt to persuade Livio to seek advancement at Court is bolstered by two references to husbands who sell or prostitute their wives and the argument is entirely materialistic. Plainly Livio's moral sense is at risk. Troylo's aside to Octavio when he enters, 'He's our own surely, nay most persuadedly' (I.1:p.141), with its echo of Livia's aside to Hippolyto after tempting Isabella to incest, 'She's your own, go', in Middleton's *Women Beware Women* (II.1), might suggest that the preceding dialogue has been engineered by Octavio for his own, and not for Troylo's pleasure. Significantly when we see him again two scenes later Livio has begun to speak Troylo's language: 'Name and honour, What are they? — mere sound without supportance' (I.3:p.152-3). In his later description of Octavio's palace as 'a little world of Fancy' (II.2:p.168), he plainly uses the word 'Fancy' in its derogatory sense, for it is here that Troylo finds it necessary to reassure him by letting him into the secret of Octavio's supposed impotence. Again there is some emphasis upon the Marquis' lecherous character at this point. 'He would now and then be piddling And play the wanton like a fly that dallies About a candle's flame' (p.169), but he is also given to 'huge jealous fits' and will allow no one to come near the Fancies more than once. For this reason and to make assurance doubly sure, he has married his barber Secco to Morosa the guardianess of the Fancies.

Now Secco, Morosa and Spadone are a trio of foul-mouthed low comedians who with the clown Nitido provide a sinister undercurrent of bawdry which skillfully underlines the purpose of the first three acts. Octavio's supposed impotence receives a lewd comment in Spadone's attempt to fasten upon

Nitido a liaison with Morosa while giving himself out to be a eunuch. Yet towards the end of the play and under Secco's threats, Spadone withdraws all his allegations including that of his own disability, while Octavio's supposed impotence is apparently forgotten. Now this development is surely a complete contradiction of the intention in the earlier action. It seems clear that Spadone was intended to seduce Morosa, throwing the blame upon the unfortunate Nitido; after what we have seen of Morosa's moral standards in the first part of the play, this late removal of suspicion is neither acceptable nor relevant.

Morosa's assurance to Castamela of Octavio's impotence is suggestive primarily in what she leaves unsaid. Her intention is significantly qualified by her description of the Fancies as 'A kind of chaste collapsed ladies', an impression scarcely softened by the following phrase — 'In their fortunes You are pregnant'. Step by step Castamela is placed unmistakably as an intended victim like Castiza in *The Revenger's Tragedy*; for what it is worth there is a touch of Vindice's anxiety for his sister in Livio's line as he watches Castamela follow the Fancies, 'Be now my sister, stand a trial bravely' (III.3:p.199).

As it stands the play bristles with queries. First, why should an experienced dramatist build up with such care and skill an impression he intended to dismiss at the end of the play? If the Ford of the first three acts really intended Castamela for Troylo how explain the almost total lack of contact between them? — not to speak of the clumsiness of Octavio's build-up of Troylo in the first scene of Act V, presumably to prepare us to accept the dénouement. Again if Troylo is really anxious to allay Livio's fears why does he not do so by revealing the less embarrassing secret of Octavio's relationship with the Fancies? If he did not know of it why not? Was it not an afterthought? If Octavio's intentions towards the Fancies are pure why does he place as their guardianess the evil-minded Morosa? Can we credit Ford with this elaborate development of the idea of impotence unless it was to have more dramatic importance than as an aid to mystification?

That Ford was writing with a clear sense of purpose is recognisable from the style as well as the overall planning of the first three acts. The dialogue is clear, swift and vigorous and the unpleasantness of the subject is evidently part of the dramatic intention. The action reaches a climax at II.3, where Castamela talks with Octavio alone. Like Bianca in *Women Beware Women* outfacing the Cardinal, Castamela denounces Octavio's conduct and, again like Bianca, suggests a remedy, exhorting him to a goodness worthy of his wealth and place.[4] Towards the end of the speech both characters falter. Plainly Castamela is moved by something in Octavio's reaction which is left to the actor:

> I am too bold Sir,
> Some anger and some pity hath directed
> A wandering trouble.
>
> (III.3:p.202)

And she promises to remain as his guest — to which Octavio answers, 'Be — but hereafter I know not what.'

Gifford describes this episode as one of great beauty; certainly its controlled feeling and delicate restraint — the half-articulate self-discovery in both characters — are characteristic of Ford's art at its most mature. There follows the curious comment of Morosa (p.203), 'All is incked[5] here. Good soul indeed' and Castamela's remark to Troylo 'You have been counsellor To a strange dialogue' (p.209). Plainly Castamela's conversation with Octavio has been overheard and there is indeed a reversal. Surely everything points to the explanation that Troylo was meant to be Octavio's procurer, not Castamela's lover. The stronger the corruption of the Court is painted, the stronger grows the impression of Castamela's innocence; and the episode in III.3 seems to be the beginning of what might well have ended in a conversion and some kind of change of life. The similarity in the build-up of the idea of corruption in Octavio's Court to that in the presentation of the Ducal Court in *The Revenger's Tragedy* is of course only one of general impression. The scope of Ford's play is narrowed by comparison, concerned with relatives, servants and backstairs underlings rather than with princes and parasites, yet it is possible that Ford's original intention was to write a tragi-comedy with the basic pattern and general moral outlook of *The Revenger's Tragedy* in mind.

If this was indeed Ford's original intention a number of other anomalies fall into place. It would explain the

impersonal relationship between Castamela and Troylo and
the curious choice of Morosa as guardianess to the Fancies. If
the Marquis conceived in the first three acts is the true one,
both sub-plots, at present broken-backed or irrelevant, have a
clear dramatic function. We have seen how Spadone's pretence
of sexual disability points to that reported of Octavio.
Meantime Flavia's loyalty to both her present husband and the
first who betrayed her and her determination to mend her
relations with her brother Romanello lend some emphasis to
the possible regenerative influence of Castamela in Octavio's
Court. Again Flavia's toying with Camillo and Vespucci after
her husband's desertion is out of keeping as the play now
stands, but it would not be unacceptable in a lively young
woman, bored as well as disillusioned, seen in the context of a
story in which the main characters are enmeshed not only in
their own vice but also in its prime consequence — a loss of
reputation which can so work upon a man that he runs into
further follies. In the play's present form slander has become a
major interest; on the other hand until after the third act it
appears to be ancillary, a contributory, not a main cause of evil
in Octavio's Court.

It seems to me that Octavio was intended to be another of
Ford's extreme cases. Jonson had used the idea of the supposedly impotent old man and the young woman prostituted
to his lust in *Volpone*. Ford was using old concepts but the
presentation of the pervert imprisoned in his own perversion
and the frankly brutal statement of the offensiveness of vice are
new. If the overstatement is perhaps barely compensated by the
artistry of the play's handling it is only fair to admit the
possibility of cuts, especially in the Flavia sub-plot. Whatever
the history of the play Ford's mind was still running on
Revenge Tragedy. It would be characteristic of Ford and
acceptable to a contemporary audience to build up the concept
of the virtuous woman trapped, like Castiza in *The Revenger's
Tragedy*, in a corrupt environment as the basis for a new
approach to domestic tragi-comedy. It was the kind of
dramatic *tour de force* which Ford often found irresistable.
The task may have presented insuperable difficulties or
perhaps more practical considerations to be faced. The
Caroline private theatre enjoyed bawdry up to a point, but
beyond certain limits it could be fastidious. Were there second

thoughts? Did the dramatist yield to a timely warning of possible trouble if the play went on as originally planned? That is Ford's secret and we are not likely to find a reliable answer. Nevertheless it is difficult to dismiss an impression of wry humour — perhaps a private joke — in the slight overemphasis in the title — 'Chaste and Noble'.

As it stands the most valuable section of the play is the story of Flavia, perhaps a little truncated but otherwise unaffected by the trick ending. If, like many of Ford's heroines at bay, Flavia seems to fly in the face of ill opinion in playing up to the amorous advances of Camillo and Vespucci in her new husband's household, she is clever enough to make use of their folly to justify herself in the eyes of Romanello, the brother whose good opinion is her passionate desire. In forcing a confession from them in his presence she succeeds in convincing him of her innocence in the sordid affair in which she has become involved. But Flavia is no patient Grissel, nor has she the stoical acceptance of Dekker's Bellafront. Flavia is an honest and high-spirited young woman caught in a compromising situation. In seeking to establish her own integrity she is a taut nerve of determination; at the same time she has the vulnerable affection combined with staunch loyalty which admits no betrayal either of herself or of those she loves. She can condemn Fabricio's behaviour with a forthrightness which leaves him no room for excuse and at the same time watch over his welfare with practical help. Her depth of feeling for him is something which no new relationship can alter — a fact which she betrays in spite of herself in the half-jocular, half-satirical plea as he leaves for a 'new world' —

> If you light on
> A parrot or a monkey that has qualities
> Of a new fashion think on me —

and he answers —

> Yes lady,
> I — I shall think on you.

                                                    (III.2:p.188)

It is one of those moments of telescoped meaning in which Ford is accomplished, and more moving than the often quoted passages in which, recalling Winnifred in *The Witch of Edmonton*, she tries to conceal her tears from Julio — 'beshrew't, the brim of your hat Struck in mine eye.[6] Her relationship with her new husband Julio who dotes upon her is an exposure of character which deserves further development. That he can deny her nothing is no security to a woman who knows from experience the fallibility of love. Flavia's handling of him may again owe something to Dekker's influence. She knows better than to push him too far, nor will she allow her 'bride price' to be added to by asking his help for Fabricio. So she dissembles her old love without violating it and gives herself to the new which so obviously deserves it. The passage in which she begs Julio to aid her reconciliation with Romanello is a convincing combination of wilfulness and tenderness with a sincerity unclouded by ulterior motive. Like most of the men in the play, Julio has the weakness of self-consciousness, She urges him to visit Romanello in order to make the first advance; but suppose he meets with peevishness? — 'Must I then petition him?' Of this endemic insecurity Flavia demands a great deal:

> Yea marry must you
> Or else you love not me ...
> Yes I will see him; so I will, will see him; —
> You hear't — Oh my good lord, dear, gentle, prithee —
> You shan't be angry ...
>   let us meet
> And talk a little.

                                                      (III.2:p.190)

The touch of hysteria, the tension between imperiousness at 'You hear't' and spontaneous affection — 'dear, gentle, prithee — You shan't be angry' — the fear lest she try his patience too far, have the natural innocence of a child combined with the passions of a woman. Flavia's marriage is not going to be easy but she will go to great lengths to make it good. After the restraint of Calantha and Lady Katherine and the pent-up feeling in Penthea and Ithocles, this is a new departure in Ford's characterisation. But it depends for its effect upon a

flexibility of verse, a movement and freedom of rhythm which
we have not seen in Ford's work before this play. It is a pity that
he did not see fit to make the story of Flavia the major interest
in this or some other drama. In embryo it is a domestic
situation of unusual complexity; the impression is of a strong
nature preserving its own integrity in a tangle of relationships
with characters dissembling, self-deceiving, self-regarding
and, by comparison, conventional and inflexible.

THE LADY'S TRIAL

The story of Flavia, Romanello, Fabricio and Julio is no mean
introduction to that of Auria, Spinella, Aurelio and Adurni in
The Lady's Trial.

'Woful satisfaction for a divorce of hearts' — Spinella's
brief but pregnant exclamation dismisses for the little they are
worth, compared with the damage they have done, the well-
meant officiousness of Aurelio, her husband's friend, in
prejudging and intruding upon her private conversation with
Adurni and, by association, the latter's high-flown excuse for
compromising Spinella as a means of testing her virtue.
Indirectly it also applies to Malfato's outraged dignity and
similar readiness to believe the worst when in the sub-plot
Levidolche attempts to court his interest. In *The Lady's Trial*
Ford exposes a number of hypocrisies in the well-bred middle
classes of his time, and in particular, the power of scandal.
Professor Anderson sees as Ford's major theme the point 'that
love should be perceptive enough to withstand misleading
appearances'.[7] But the play's meaning goes deeper, I think,
than this; it explores the stresses and strains within the
individual, not only at the onslaught of scandal, but also
under the pressures of a sophisticated social code.

Auria, a Genoese nobleman and a skilled soldier, has
married a young and beautiful, but dowerless wife, Spinella.
As the play opens he determines to rebuild his finances by
offering his services to the Duke of Florence against the Turks,
a proposal which meets with the stern disapproval of his
friend Aurelio who has never entirely countenanced his
marriage with so young and impoverished a bride. In Auria's
absence Spinella visits, in company with her sister Castanna

and Aurelio, the house of the young lord Adurni. While there Adurni contrives to entertain Spinella alone; she resists his advances, but Aurelio breaks in upon them and denounces them both — and Spinella disappears.

At this point Auria returns from the wars, covered with success and glory, to find his wife missing and the object of scandal. Auria challenges Aurelio to prove his charge; Aurelio can only stand by what he has done but their altercation is cut short by the arrival of Castanna with news of Spinella. She has taken refuge with Malfato, her cousin, who secretly loves her but has never declared himself. The main plot ends in a 'trial' scene in which Aurelio and Adurni make their defence and Spinella, hurt and indignant at her husband's apparent harsh judgement of her, passes through a gamut of emotions to a final collapse. Whereupon Auria accepts the fact of her innocence and seals his faith in her by arranging a marriage between Castanna and Adurni.

There are two sub-plots. In the first Levidolche, niece to Martino, has like Auria made an apparent mismarriage — with Benatzi, a serving-man. The marriage has been annulled and Levidolche has begun to take lovers, among them Lord Adurni, who tires of her; whereupon she turns to a more serious attraction in Malfato, who indignantly rejects her. Meantime Benatzi returns disguised as an old soldier, is aided by Levidolche and swears to avenge her. She has however seen through his disguise, the pair are reconciled and remarry. The second sub-plot is pure farce. It concerns Amoretta, the young, affected — and snobbish — daughter of Trecaltio, with high notions of social status and a persistent lisp. The loquacious and ever-ready attendants upon Adurni, Piero and Futelli, offer their ingenuity to 'cure' Amoretta by staging a dual courtship by two upstarts, a Genoese impecunious gallant and a Spanish adventurer, disguised respectively as a Prince and a Don. A good deal of slapstick comedy and some obvious but not ineffective satire arises out of their advances to Amoretta, the more comic in that the indefatigable agents have persuaded them both of the reality of their superimposed identity. When they are exposed and kicked rudely from the stage, Amoretta repents, forgets her passion for 'crownths' and 'pinthes' and submits to her father's will in accepting Futelli as her husband.

To a great extent the main plot repeats the pattern of *A Woman Killed with Kindness.* On Auria's return we have again the aggrieved husband, the apparently erring wife, the wrong done to their relationship by the friend, combined with the real assault upon the wife's virtue by a mutual friend. Aurelio expects Auria to take revenge as Nicholas, the loyal servant, expects of Frankford in Heywood's play, and we are not allowed to forget that all this is happening in Italy where swift and bloody reprisal may be expected for wounded honour. But to the domestic tragic pattern Ford poses the question — suppose the wife is innocent, suppose the well-intentioned informer is mistaken, and suppose the husband should look for another means of clearing his reputation than either killing the wife of friend or wringing the penitent's heart-strings? In a situation where neither side is guilty except of misjudgement, and even the would-be seducer is good enough at heart to warrant the husband's admitting him to his own family, the 'trial' becomes less one of virtue than of character.

Auria's folly in leaving Spinella so soon after their marriage is stressed at the beginning of the play, but it is worth noting by whom — by Piero and Futelli who assess everything by the amusement and comfort it can afford, and then by Aurelio who takes the conventional view, not only of Auria's present purpose but of his marriage in itself. Marriage for Aurelio is for a man's advancement; if he can combine advancement with love, so much the better, but to marry for love alone is a sin against discretion and will damage 'opinion'. In his self-righteous sense of propriety Aurelio does not notice the slight irony of Auria's reply — 'I find it hath' — and proceeds to point out the further folly of leaving a young bride exposed to temptation. The importance of this expository dialogue to the meaning of the play can hardly be over-estimated. In Aurelio's judgement all young wives are fallible, all mere love relationships suspect; his mind is fertile soil for ill conception and Spinella is half judged already. The situation becomes more ominous when Auria, firmly dismissing suppositions for more practical matters, leaves Spinella's financial arrangements in the hands of so over-zealous a friend.

At Aurelio's next appearance (I.3) we find him proffering unwelcome advice to Malfato, whose settled melancholy he believes he can probe. In such cases, he says, a friend may be 'the best physician, for admit We find no remedy we cannot miss Advice instead of comfort'. Aurelio is the typical self-constituted counsellor; he is also the would-be guardian of the social order, for later in the scene he rebukes Malfato for sneering at rank — 'Make all men equal and confound the course Of order and of nature!' Aurelio's convictions generally contain a modicum of truth, but like Gregers Werle in *The Wild Duck*, a character similarly afflicted with 'rectitudinitis', he is destined to bring ill-luck. But like Auria, Malfato puts him off gently; with all his clumsiness there is something appealing in Aurelio — he has simply mistaken discretion for wisdom.

The first impression of Spinella, in the scene of Auria's departure, is of a 'gracious silence':

Faith, purity of thoughts and such a meekness
As would force scandal to a blush ...

(I.1:p.259)

To Auria Spinella is invulnerable; but the mention of scandal is functional. If Aurelio pays too much attention to it, Auria pays too little. When Spinella breaks her silence to express her natural fears for his safety and for her own happiness, the implication is that her innocence has given her a clearer insight than Auria's experience of the world has conferred on him. There is, however, some emphasis upon slight indiscretions in Spinella's conduct during Auria's absence. To begin with Auria spends some time exhorting her to caution — not only to be virtuous but to be seen to be so. Later it is surely with some deliberation that Piero and Futelli are made to refer briefly to Spinella's gambling losses. Since the matter is never mentioned again it is obviously meant to be noticed, but in relation to background rather than character. It suggests that eyes are on Spinella and that minor indiscretions are likely to be exaggerated.[8] But the contrast with Heywood's Lucrece, who blames herself for allowing so much candle-light about the house in her husband's absence, is nevertheless striking. Ford's heroine is a woman and a very natural one!

The real Spinella, the being whose unassailable innocence moves Adurni to worship, we see in the latter's house. When the full realisation of Adurni's intentions dawns upon her Spinella has no denunciation, no virtuous vituperation, only a passionate plea to his better nature. In the often-quoted evocation of Auria there is a good deal of realism —

> Fight not for name abroad, but come my husband,
> Fight for thy wife at home —
>
> (II.4:p.292)

and the damage which a blemished name can do to the freedom of her spirit is plainly stated in her last line to Adurni before Aurelio intrudes upon them — 'Make not your house my prison.'

Spinella's flight is a concession to her fears which she will have to repudiate later, but she does not leave without a shaft of irony. Her accusation that the episode will furnish Aurelio 'with some news for entertainment' and that her removal from Auria's affections will knit his own relationship with him the faster, gets no answer, but that it has been voiced prepares for the final scene in which the tables will be turned and it is Aurelio who will place himself in the wrong.

So Spinella passes on to yet another man of principle — Malfato, her melancholy cousin. The scene between Malfato and Spinella (IV.1.) is perhaps the most delicately handled in the play. It opens with his sympathetic but close questioning as to what precisely happened in Adurni's house, to which Spinella's straightforward replies evidently move him to reveal his own love for her which he has held in check since before her marriage. Now we have seen Malfato harshly assuming, on receiving a letter from Levidolche by Adurni's attendants, that she is offering herself to his use on Adurni's defection; we have also heard from Martino, Levidolche's uncle, of his contemptuous reference to her in public. It is in keeping that now Spinella, also destitute, has turned to him for protection, he should confess that convention, the fear of propinquity of blood, inhibited him from speaking at the right time — 'he durst not — because he durst not.' Yet the same man can take advantage of Spinella's trust in him to reveal his feeling for her now. Spinella tactfully accepts the story, told in the third person, of his hapless love but her reaction to it is with the artlessness of childhood — 'Twas wonderful.' The temptation implied in his confession, such as might have moved Levidolche to the ultimate folly, Spinella simply does not hear; the effect is to turn Malfato's ill-timed passion into a determination to defend her good name — 'By noble love made jealous of her fame'. When Castanna enters with the news of Auria's return her anxiety as to what he will think of her breaks from her in a rush of speech not far from tears:

> Oh prithee do not hear me call him husband,
> Before thou canst resolve what kind of wife
> His fury terms the runaway; speak quickly.
> Yet do not — stay, Castanna I am lost!
>
> (IV.1:p.321)

There follows a typical moment of dialogue recalling in its dramatic succinctness and verbal echo the Duke's challenge in *Love's Sacrifice* (IV.1:p.347). To Castanna's assurance that Auria laughs at the charges laid against her Spinella replies in two arresting monosyllables — 'Does he?' After her excited questioning this brief phrase suggests a complexity of feeling beyond verbal expression. The whole episode, with its exposure of pent emotion and gentle withdrawal, is designed to demonstrate the therapeutic power over other characters of Spinella's innocence. It also builds up the impression that the same innocence can nevertheless have its pejorative effect, that what lies now between Spinella and Auria is less a matter of slander than one of shamefastness and consequent failure in mutual trust.

In the closer look it gives us at Malfato the episode also underlines the fallibility of Aurelio's principles. The melancholic and the moralist are curiously alike. Both are awkward men of impeccable intentions. As Aurelio condemns Spinella on the flimsiest of indiscretions, so does Malfato condemn Levidolche as the prostitute her fundamental goodness of heart could never permit her to be. It is with the same inflexible judgement that Aurelio presents the situation to Auria on his return.

There are many precedents in Jacobean drama for embarrassments between two well-meaning and trusty friends. The pattern had been well worked over by Beaumont and

Fletcher — between Maximus and Aecius in *Valentinian* and
Amintor and Melantius in *The Maid's Tragedy*. In both cases
the debate is between honour on the one hand and loyalty of a
subject to an unjust sovereign on the other; in both episodes
swords are drawn and sheathed, in both the dialogue peters out
in high-minded face-saving, a situation which Middleton
gently parodied in the duel scene, also between trusted friends,
in *A Fair Quarrel*.[9] Ford's departure from what had become a
theatrical tradition is striking. Aurelio justifies himself by
declaring that what he did was done in honour and good faith
and counsels Auria to exact the conventional price of honour
— revenge. Auria answers 'for what?', and all the evidence
Aurelio can produce when put to it is 'But I broke ope the
doors upon them'. Their exchanges have a touch of humour,
the more so as we see Auria's rising anger tempered with sheer
irritability. Auria's protest that had Aurelio 'stayed wisely
silent' he could have challenged Adurni himself, and his
violent cry — 'I make demand my wife! — you — sir' as he
draws his sword, have suggested to some critics that Auria is
not entirely convinced of Spinella's innocence. If this is Ford's
intention the doubt is immediately removed when Castanna
enters to rebuke Aurelio for his conduct, and dismissed
altogether by his later acceptance of Adurni. With Castanna's
revelation Auria's anger melts, not because he will not draw on
a friend who means well if mistakenly, but because Aurelio's
persistent defence not only of his intention but of the
righteousness of his action is turning the situation into farce:

> Again hear and believe it,
> What I have done was well done and well meant.
>
> (III.3:p.311)

With so honest a man to fight would be 'dotage'; rather let
them join forces to 'listen after this straying soul', and Aurelio
responds with encouragement. 'Why there's a friend now' is
Auria's final comment. Auria's good sense is as therapeutic as
Spinella's innocence, and when Castanna enters to challenge
Aurelio on her own account, her cool judgement of the affair,
her sensible rebuke that he was 'not very kind to me either' help
to put him in the wrong as no heroic expression of outrage
could. Ford can do without sententiousness, or an appeal to an

abstract ideal or to the claims of one kind of honour above another. This is a piece of sheer realism, closer to Middleton or Shakespeare than to Fletcher or the Caroline dramatists.

Ford's preparation for the final confrontation of husband and wife is worth watching. With every challenge Aurelio's dramatic stature dwindles and meantime Spinella's grows. In the scene between the two friends and Adurni (IV.2) Aurelio is left with nothing but the good intention of which we have heard so much, but Adurni's confession with its proud frankness throws new light on Spinella. Again the 'power of virtue', the 'commanding sovereignty' of Spinella's innocence is testified to, but it is significant that when Adurni speaks of her person it is not in the high-flown praise of beauty, familiar in Ford's theatre and parodied in Guzman's evocation of Amoretta (III.r.), but in terms of human quality:

> I found a woman good; — a woman good! ...
>   so much majesty
> Of humbleness and scorn, appeared at once
> In fair, in chaste, in wise Spinella's eyes.
>
> (IV.2:p.336)

In the focus of the play Spinella has developed from the child wife of the first act into a woman of poise and authority.

Auria does not yet show his hand, but his withdrawal from the conversation to think out some plan which, he mutters, 'smooths all rubs' is a clear indication that the solution will be happy. Ford's dislike of surprise for its own sake is surely obvious in this careful reinstatement of Adurni in the audience's eyes, but the fact that, while Auria's intentions appear to be therapeutic, we do not know precisely how he will carry them out, builds up dramatic tension towards his meeting with Spinella in the final scene.

Spinella makes her first mistake in kneeling — an action she condemns later as 'faintness and stupidity'. When Auria on his part, still smarting under her avoidance of him, pretends not to recognise her he makes a gesture symbolic of the gulf that has come between them. But to the more conventional Malfato it is a piece of 'antic sovereignty' which he sarcastically rebukes — 'You know your wife no doubt.'. The altercation goads Spinella into recollection of her true self. From a false meekness she passes to a fierce resistance; while anyone can find 'a likelihood of guilt' in her behaviour she will have none of him or any of her kindred, at which Auria ironically applauds her new 'masculine' confidence. The lash of his derision does its work; Spinella finds in it the stimulus to challenge Aurelio on her own level — 'Speak, sir, the churlish voice of this combustion, Aurelio speak' — for it is his 'canker'd falsehood' that has wrought 'so foul a mischief'; and Malfato notes with approval, 'He's put to't; It seems the challenge gravels him.' Aurelio's last flicker of self-justification, that the removal of suspicion often knits relationships more closely, is exposed for the pretence that it is by Spinella's flash of realism — 'Woeful satisfaction for a divorce of hearts' (V.2:p.347).

Apart from this everything Spinella has said so far is coloured by her obsession with the power of public opinion, while the compulsion of truth is vibrant as much in what Auria does not say as in the splendid irony which runs through the dialogue. Now it is Auria's turn for eloquence; he will 'touch nearer home', and thereupon he reminds her that in spite of differences in years and fortune, 'Love drove the bargain' of their union 'and the truth of love Confirmed it', to which Spinella replies, still with the idea of severance in her mind, that such love suspected 'without or ground or witness' is more deserving of a separation than downright frailty. When Adurni enters to ask pardon of Spinella, implying that all those present are as misguided as he has been, there is a certain relish in the use Auria makes of his intervention — 'Baited by confederacy! I must have right.' The word 'right' causes Spinella to face Auria squarely at last — with his own kind of truth, a truth tempered by reason and humanity but, most important, a truth to herself:

> And I, my lord, my lord —
> What stir and coil is here! You can suspect?
> So reconciliation then is needless ...
>
> I have assumed a courage
> Above my force and can hold out no longer.
> Auria, unkind, unkind!

                                                        (p.349)

In thus stressing the physical and emotional effects of
Spinella's ordeal, Ford is perhaps deliberately recalling the
collapse of Heywood's Mrs Frankford and Mrs Wincott.
Ford's heroine dies only to her own shamefastness and her
vulnerability to the pressures of a sophisticated society. In this
delicately conceived dialogue Aurelio's half-realised theory is
in fact proved. We are left in little doubt that there has been a
weakness at the heart of Auria's union with Spinella — the
point at which conventional assumptions of conduct can
damage a relationship otherwise perfectly attuned. But
although the damaging power of 'misleading appearances'[10]
in human intercourse is a major interest, I cannot agree that it
is the main theme of the play. Spinella's trial penetrates deeper
than conjugal faith or the effect of public opinion upon it.
Auria's function is rather to probe like a psychiatrist than to
assess like a judge and the test involves other major characters
with her. Auria's rough handling demonstrates that ill
suspicion could have no power over Spinella did not
shamefastness and false pride inhibit both her truth to
herself and her confidence in her husband's faith in her.
Aurelio and Malfato make their disastrous misjudgements
not because they are given to thinking evil, but because their
minds are conditioned by a social code which, for the first
time, they are forced to question. Ford's recurrent theme of the
violation of human integrity receives a new twist here in that,
in the purview of the play, such a violation can happen from
within as well as from without, and in the closest of human
ties. It was a new aspect of the theme which could most aptly
be presented through the medium of domestic drama, but it
necessitated taking the action deeper into the complexities
that lie at the root of human relationships and their reaction
upon the mind and the emotions than he had ever penetrated
before.

After witnessing Auria's gift in marriage of Castanna to
Adurni — Auria's way of settling a debt of honour — the
audience would no doubt enjoy the entrance of Benatzi,
brandishing a sword and roaring for vengeance upon Adurni
and Malfato for their insulting treatment of his new-found
wife Levidolche, only to be disarmed in mind as well as in act
by the kindly authority of Auria. It is a piece of comic irony
underlining the victory of reason and humanity over

conventional honour and prejudice, to which the slant of the whole play has been pointing.

Instances of a teasing, tongue-in-the-cheek humour are a distinguishing mark of this play. Auria's firm but fundamentally good-humoured challenge to the high-mindedness of the two people he values most implies a gently ironic, but nevertheless penetrating comment on the fashionable idealism of some of his younger colleagues in the Caroline theatre;[11] it is also a departure from Perkin Warbeck's humourless constancy and Calantha's stoical continence. The latter are both aspects of integrity but the implication of this play is that conviction may not be enough. A man comes to full maturity when he can call upon reason and understanding to guide his conduct and assess his vision of truth. This, I think, would be Ford's conception of wisdom.

The Lady's Trial is an impressive and unusual play, but it nevertheless falls short of mastery. Throughout the last act the dramatist seems to be consciously — and not without difficulty — holding the natural expression of feeling in leash. During the trial scene Auria is either teasing or stern — never tender — and when at last he reveals himself there is no natural reconciliation, no spontaneous joy, only a factual proof of his faith in his offer of his sister-in-law to Adurni. In his final words to Spinella we have a comment upon behaviour, none upon the feelings, and even that is tempered with a little blame for her flight, 'To whom my love and nature were no strangers'. He could have said as much to Adurni and Malfato, we have heard him express much more to Aurelio. Ford's determination to avoid the sententiousness of Heywood's domestic tragedy seems to cut short the situation so carefully built towards its climax. The main plot is the skeleton of a very good play, but as it is, the lack of sufficient material for five acts has to be compensated in the sub-plots. The relevance of the Levidolche story has been commented upon, but even here a scene between that vividly presented young woman and Malfato might have been of value. Credibility has to be strained to see any link with the main plot, of the 'curing' of Amoretta. Apart from its touches of satire this part of the play is kept alive only by the presence of that untiring pair of ingenious plotters and gossips, Futelli and Piero. It is a surprising falling off in the author of *The Broken Heart* and *Perkin Warbeck*.

Yet the care which Ford lavished on what was probably his last play is borne out in the variety of its style. Nowhere else in his plays does he take such pains to make the manner reflect the character or the mood. In the opening scene (I.1:p.255) Piero and Futelli parody the bombast of heroic drama: 'Accomplished man of fashion! ... The time's wonder, Gallant of gallants ... Italy's darling, Europe's joy and so forth', with perhaps a malicious side-glance at Webster — 'Is all my signior's hospitality shrunk ... To beverage and biscuit?'[12] Later the sham Spanish Don and the supposed Prince use the hyperbole of the roles imposed upon them as background for the childish prattle, no less superimposed, of the lisping Amoretta. In contrast Martino and Levidolche sling talk at one another with a forthrightness fundamental to their natures and to their function in the play.

Between the main characters communication is not so easy. When we see Auria, Aurelio and Spinella for the first time all three are either aggrieved or embarrassed — Aurelio condemning, on a delicate and personal matter, Auria feeling himself condemned, Spinella striving for courage and a stoicism she was not born to. It is noticeable that all three speak in a curiously involved style, first heard in Lady Katherine's carefully worded reply to Dalyell's confession of love, but used in this play when the characters have a problem of tact or self-control to reckon with. For instance Malfato uses the same style of speech to reveal his feelings for Spinella whereas, because her mind only half registers what he is saying, Spinella's replies are brief and simple. When Auria returns from the wars the tension is all on Aurelio's part and Auria's direct statements and challenging questions are in clear contrast with his friend's long-winded attempts at self-justification for his treatment of Spinella. Aurelio talks in abstraction, in circumlocution, in indirect metaphor:

> No Auria, I dare vie with your respects;
> Put both into the balance and the poise
> Shall make a settled stand: perhaps the proffer
> So frankly vowed at your departure first,
> Of settling me a partner in your purchase,
> Leads you into opinion of some ends
> Of mercenary falsehood ...

> (III.3:p.309)

Auria's reply to these lines throws their pretentiousness into relief:

> By all my sorrows
> The mention is too coarse.

But when Auria draws his sword in an outburst of rage and grief, Aurelio throws off his embarrassment to speak some of the most lucid and emphatic lines in the play:

> What I have done was well done and well meant;
> Twenty times over, were it new to do,
> I'd do't and do't, and boast the pains religious.
>
> (p.311)

This sudden and natural change under stress from involvement to plainness can have its comic side. When Auria pretends not to recognise Spinella as she kneels to him, Malfato stands by, a prey to confusion as well as indignation:

> My lord you use a borrow'd bravery,
> Not suiting fair constructions: may your fortunes
> Mount higher than can apprehension reach 'em!
> Yet this waste kind of antic sovereignty
> Unto a wife who equals every best
> Of your deserts, achievements or prosperity,
> Bewrays a barrenness of noble nature.
>
> (V.2:p.345)

Malfato is too honest not to speak his mind at this point, yet the phrases 'borrowed bravery', 'fair constructions', 'every best of your deserts' cloud the meaning with words; but as Malfato's indignation mounts his gentlemanly embarrassment collapses to expose the nonsense of Auria's assumed attitude in the line quoted above — 'You know your wife no doubt.' As is usual in Ford's work when play of character is in question, a great deal depends upon the vocal tone, the pace and the general approach of the actor.

Throughout the episode Spinella's speeches are vibrant with pent-up feeling which at one point seems to be held in check by the same involvement. Auria has reminded Spinella

of their marriage with, this time, a gentler challenge —
'Speak your thoughts.' Spinella is moved but her love is at a
tension with her wounded dignity. Her thoughts she says, are
as his,

> yet herein evidence of frailty
> Deserv'd not more a separation
> Than doth charge of disloyalty objected
> Without ground or witness.

(p.348)

Again the meaning loses itself in verbal meanderings, yet the
same Spinella can attack, a few moments later, the confusion
which she feels overwhelming her —

> What stir and coil is here! you can suspect? ...
> Auria unkind, unkind!

(p.349)

The artifice in which the serious characters seem to take refuge
is unusual, but this flexibility of manner to the passing mood
is something one would have liked to see developed in a more
finished play.

But while *The Lady's Trial* has its faults and probably
suffers from some weakness in its original planning, it is one
of Ford's most valuable contributions to the Caroline stage.
For it demonstrates the effectiveness in poetic drama of the rub
of one character upon another, of the variety and fragility of
human relationships, of the depth and complexity of human
motivation. It is this sensitivity to the dynamism within the
individual personality and the unpredictable in human
behaviour that in Ford's hands turns the outworn
sententiousness of domestic drama into comic irony. This is
Ford's substitute for the overplayed social satire to which the
Prologue to the play makes a slighting reference — 'Wit, wit's
the word in fashion, that alone Cries up the poet.'[13]

A feature of this play is the variety and extent of the uses to
which every permanent amenity of the stage is put and in
particular the use of the stage entrances. As the play opens
Piero and Futelli enter 'at opposite doors' each bringing with
him his own pupil in the plot surrounding Amoretta. Another

stage direction reads 'Enter on the opposite side Fulgoso and Piero to Guzman and Futelli' (II.1). The doors at the sides of the stage, not those in the stage front, were probably used for these entrances with some comic effect. The same doors must have been used in several street scenes when characters pass over the stage. But the door used for Aurelio's dramatic incursion to Adurni and Spinella (II.3) must have been the central double door in the stage front so that attention could be centred upon him.

This climax in the episode in Adurni's house (II.3) is worth following for its stage management. Two scenes earlier in a street scene (II.1) Adurni's expected guests pass over the stage and are noted by Fulgoso and Guzman, presumably downstage. There follows a scene in Martino's house long enough to reveal the background news of Malfato's ill opinion of Levidolche and Auria's successful return. The characters probably entered for this scene through the closed hangings to one side of the stage. In the short scene which follows we are in Adurni's house; again the characters enter through the hangings and Piero draws Amoretta's attention to 'the next gallery' (the upper stage?) and conducts Amoretta and Castanna away — possibly to the upper stage (where they remain until Aurelio's noisy entrance, when they follow on his heels). After this preparation Adurni's contrivance is ready — 'a song within' and 'a banquet set out'. The hangings part centre stage, revealing the banquet as a visual focus of interest. The whole act is planned as an extended locality, using in its course the entire stage area, the actors moving easily from one imagined meeting-place to another, all contrived by simply varying the entrances and exits. But Ford clearly required this flexibility not only for its practical usefulness but also to keep the rest of the action in mind as a build-up to this crisis in Spinella's relations with her husband. It is a development from the staging of the balancing scenes in England and Scotland in *Perkin Warbeck*.

Another interesting episode is that in Trecaltio's house (IV.2) where for Amoretta's childish pleasure music and later a song are heard 'below' although the characters are all assembled on the main stage. Was this music performed below the side of the stage — at audience level — or beneath it? There is no certain evidence of a 'cellerage' under the stage either at

Blackfriars or the Phoenix, although it is probable that Inigo Jones provided for a carpeted space under the stage at the reconstructed Royal Cockpit and of course most of the large open theatres built in Elizabethan times had possessed an under-stage level and one or more traps. But since this is the only instance in Ford's surviving plays of the use of an under-stage level it seems hardly likely that such constructions were provided at the Phoenix. While Ford's demands upon the stage are comparatively simple they grow with experience and in his plays for the Phoenix he generally requires a full and flexible use of all the available aids to dramatic production.

The Lady's Trial is little known and seldom included in selected editions of Ford's plays. This is regrettable, for it offers particular opportunities and challenges for the actor. In characterisation and motive, above all in the variety of tone and style in the dialogue, the play requires the speaking voice and the rapport between stage and audience to release its quality. In every way this is a play for a small audience in the intimate surroundings of the Phoenix. Yet for the student of drama the play's emphasis upon reason and urbanity has more in common with the Restoration than the Caroline theatre, Fundamentally and in spite of its late place in the Ford canon, *The Lady's Trial* was a potential new beginning.

8 The Challenge of the Caroline Theatre

It cannot be stressed too often that if we are to understand what life and work in the Caroline theatre were like we must rid ourselves of our own historical hindsight. Never since the drama became secular had the companies and the dramatists who wrote for them known such professional status or such reliable protection. Elizabeth had remained aloof from tensions between the theatres and the Puritan party, James had given his patronage and, in ordering alterations to the Cockpit-in-Court so that plays could be performed there, Prince Henry had shown a practical interest. But with Charles and his Queen the royal family were not only actively interested in drama but were seen to be so. For the time being Puritan opposition could be safely ignored.

The leading London companies, with the hope of an invitation to play at Court before them, might be expected to give of their best to a worthwhile play, not only in acting but in decor, costume, lighting and general staging. There was no lack of opportunity for an author with initiative and a certain degree of tolerance. Even the rivalry of the amateur playwright at Court or at the Inns of Court had its healthier side. Despite Ben Jonson's persistent complaints the importance of the dramatist in a team of experts for a dramatic performance was clearly established. Suckling and Cartwright were poets of stature and if their success was partly the result of their ability to please a sophisticated taste, taste can be cajoled and even sometimes led! Fickle and shallow as the average audience might be, its devotion to fashion could suggest a need for direction, and in the intimate atmosphere of the private theatre the spectators were raw material for a vigorous artist with the courage of his own convictions to work upon.

For those who looked beyond the contemporary situation — back into the past or forward into an undefined future — for Jonson, Chapman, Heywood and others — there were misgivings. To them the gulf between the popular and the private theatres was no doubt the outward sign of the gulf

150

between the Elizabethan and the Caroline drama. Chapman, writing only a few reactionary tragedies after the end of the previous reign, had quietly withdrawn, Marston had left the stage for the Church, Heywood, now ageing and with his reputation established, seems to have given his energies in the Caroline period to the writing of civic pageants. Jonson was still a leading playwright and later plays such as *The Staple of News* and *The Magnetic Lady* contain some of the finest, and bitterest, satire of the time; but behind the sumptuousness of Jonson's raillery can be sensed a deep unhappiness. For Jonson drama had taken a wrong direction and as far as he himself was concerned it was now too late to turn back. He remained a lonely and resistant figure.

On the whole Ford's younger colleagues in the Caroline theatre seemed ready to meet its challenge if only to make a living. Massinger, Brome, Shirley and Davenant were producing a considerable body of drama, but all of them seemed dogged by the problem first of producing work which might prove acceptable by Court standards, secondly of providing something fresh but not too new, for their already satiated audiences. No one could better tell a story or get a plot moving than Massinger. In such plays as *The Roman Actor* and *A New Way to pay Old Debts* there is a sense of an artist's satisfaction. He could be ruthlessly frank; for instance in *The Roman Actor* the Empress' persistent meddling with the actors and her total misunderstanding of their art suggest a side-glance at the Queen, and there is a good deal of implied political comment behind the often predictable convolutions of his plots, but the obligation to please often seems to cut short a fully realised artistic purpose. Nevertheless Massinger's stately line and innate reserve lend to his plays a strength which the theatre needed.

There is a toughness about the best of Brome's work and an incisiveness in his satire. But in romantic tragi-comedy — *The Queen and the Concubine* and *The Queen's Exchange* for instance — Brome seems to lavish his energies on themes and intrigues derived from the romances, to please a popular fancy while it lasted. Both he and Shirley were accomplished poet-dramatists and Shirley in particular knew how to curb the emotionalism their audiences loved. Yet both give the impression of a holding back from living human experience;

in both there is a sense of compromise. Apart from Ford, of the greater dramatists of the period only Davenant seems to have enjoyed the situation. There is a bluffness about Davenant's comedies and his plots have a bold freshness the more entertaining for a tongue-in-cheek humour and a pleasant touch of irresponsibility.

Unlike Jonson, Ford evidently had sufficient faith in the Caroline theatre to believe that a better phase of development was possible, not by retreating or complying but by fusing what was of value in the new drama with what was best in the old, so as to bring a new virility to the contemporary stage. His major achievement was in reconciling both traditional and contemporary dramatic themes with an analysis of human character, no doubt stimulated but by no means dominated by a new psychology as influential in his day as that of Freud has been in ours. Professor Stavig warns us against overemphasising the psychological as against the thematic aspect of Ford's work,[1] but in this problem of balance Ford himself is the best guide. He knew well enough an audience's capacity for apprehension and the point of saturation in its interest, and his skill in flattening or distancing certain characters to allow a theme to develop without destroying its psychological depth is a striking feature of his art. Ford had worked with the last of the Elizabethans and some of the leading Jacobean dramatists; in date he stood on the edge of a period in which a new society would dominate art and thought. No one was in a better position to understand the situation in the contemporary theatre in its true perspective or to know how to adapt what that theatre had to offer to his own purpose.

It is with all this in mind that his apparently limited scope should be judged. Because Ford seldom presented the common man it has been too readily assumed that he lacked the ability to do so. The answer is in the exchanges between Bassanes and his mumbling servants in *The Broken Heart* and the scene of Bergetto's death in *'Tis Pity She's a Whore*; the dialogue between Putana and Vasques in the latter play could have come out of Middleton. His choice of the sensitive, the cultured and well-bred as major characters was primarily, as we have seen, to suit his dramatic intention, but it was also determined to a great extent by the demands of the theatre and the indirect influence of the Court. To meet the one and challenge the other necessarily conditioned his choice of principal figures, but the overall impression after reading through the plays is that Ford wrote and planned as he did because his themes demanded it.

The charge of conservatism is superficial; there is nothing automatic about his selection of one dramatic pattern after another. Ford chose the lyrical motive of the lost and found in *The Lover's Melancholy*, the Revenge pattern in three distinctive forms in the three tragedies which followed, the historical play in *Perkin Warbeck* and the domestic tragi-comedy in *The Lady's Trial* because he found these forms best suited to the themes of the respective plays as they grew up in his mind, but once the theme had found its pattern Ford made of it something new and peculiar to himself. But it was also something which he believed the contemporary theatre could absorb and perhaps build upon. He was too much a theatre man to miss the indications of a wrong turning in the drama of his day, nor did he lack the courage to demonstrate that there was still time to turn back. But his fusion of old and new went far deeper than compromise. In his hands the Caroline audience was being cajoled into accepting new versions of current idealism carried to such logical extremes as to expose their fallacy — and this within the traditional conceptions of tragedy and tragi-comedy which had proved their viability on the Elizabethan and Jacobean stage.

Ford was always to some degree an iconoclast and in this respect his reassessment of moral sanctions deserves a further comment. The claim that we have in Ford an exponent of the traditional moral order seems to me an overstatement. The two clearest examples of tensions between the individual and the established moral order are in *'Tis Pity* and *Perkin Warbeck*. By ethical standards Giovanni is clearly in the wrong but that is not what the play is about. Similarly Perkin Warbeck's insistence upon his claim to the throne is an offence against reason and the social order; it is also an offence against truth according to the verdict of history. But as in the case of Giovanni, so in that of Warbeck, the slant of the action is on the hero's conviction and his loyalty to himself; concern for the established order, whether moral or social, is only ancillary to the purpose of the play. Ford's dislike of the pretensions of current neo-Platonism, his contempt for the prejudices and conventions of sophisticated society were equalled only by the implied criticism of representatives of the Establishment which runs through *'Tis Pity* and *Perkin Warbeck*. Yet condemnation in *The Broken Heart* of violence as a means of restoring a just balance is combined with an impartiality of treatment which throws the emphasis upon the quality of constancy instead of that of revenge in the face of adversity, and the interest in *Love's Sacrifice* is with the conflict that destroys the lovers rather than with the problem of right and wrong. To convey all this to the upper and middle-class audience at the Phoenix and Blackfriars was no easy task. It was for this reason, I believe, that Ford chose to shock his theatre into awareness of a human problem by presenting it as a deliberate overstatement; for instance Giovanni's defence of incestuous love and the symbolic heart and dagger which embody his final challenge, Bianca's offering of herself to her lover upon a desperate condition, Calantha's unnatural if stoical resistance to outward shows of grief. Defence of the traditional moral order may be implied here and there, but this was not Ford's specific purpose; rather he constantly sought a means of expression of what seems to have been a basic need in his own day — the need for stability in the individual and in the community. To demonstrate this need through the motives of revenge, jealousy and ambition, of love, lust and betrayal, in fact through the primitive passions as well as the material concerns of human beings in whom self-awareness and apprehension of contacts and tensions in daily living were well developed, was to combine nature with nurture in a manner which anticipated Dryden. Ford's tragedies have more in common with *All for Love* and *Don Sebastian* than with the plays of Brome or Shirley or William Cartwright.

But unlike Dryden and in spite of his love of extremes, Ford had little use for the concept of evil. With the exception of D'Avolos in *Love's Sacrifice* there are no evil characters as such in Ford's work, but there are plenty of erring ones. The witty observation that in Ford's plays we 'assist at the conversion of the seven deadly sins, not at their overthrow'[2] is particularly apt in relation to *The Lover's Melancholy*, *The Broken Heart* and *The Lady's Trial*. But it is the awkwardness of the high-minded and well-meaning that holds his interest; for instance the misjudgements of Huntley, of Aurelio, of Ithocles. Ford's most virtuous characters are often most accident prone!

Ford's psychological method, whether he learnt it from Burton or Dekker or Shakespeare, brings to his characterisation an empathy, a witholding from judgement which, paradoxically, has at times a chilling effect and in which in his own age he seems to have been unique. Whether misguided or not — and Ford is often deliberately vague on the matter — the characters are generally sincere according to their own lights; they may communicate in abstractions or, occasionally, by pointing to crude fact, but they also speak from the heart, a phrase which has more meaning applied to the plays of Ford than those of most of his contemporaries.

It is odd that Joan Sargeaunt should see so little humour in Ford,[3] an opinion often shared by those who nevertheless find his irony impressive. To my mind Ford's humour, sly, gentle, always implied and generally expressed as a trick of personality, is of equal dramatic value with his irony. Ford never sees his characters impaled on their own follies; he does see them a little, often lovably comic. The effect in several climatic scenes in *The Lady's Trial* depends a good deal upon this delicate humour, it goes to the making of the Huntley/Dalyell relationship in *Perkin Warbeck*, and in *The Broken Heart* the half-comic handling of Bassanes counterbalances the starkness of Penthea's misery. This was a rare element in serious drama of Ford's time — indeed for its fullest impression a better vehicle might be the novel — and the more significant in that the themes, the shape of the plays and the social background of the characters are those of traditional drama.

This kind of writing lays a great deal of responsibility on the actor and the director. In the freedom which he gives to both Ford is perhaps more modern than Caroline. With the minimum of soliloquy and only rare instances of characters reporting of one another, motive and meaning are generally to be gathered from dialogue, so that what may at first sight suggest unsureness of purpose may be a deliberate invitation to stage and audience to draw their own conclusions. Instances are the vexed queries as to the precise nature of Bianca's intentions towards her lover, of Ithocles' motives in courting Calantha, of Lady Katherine's real view of Warbeck's claim to the throne, of Auria's attitude to Spinella's conduct. It is in the multidimensional nature of Ford's art that his plays are open to a variety of interpretations; essentially they belong to the theatre and demand powers of vocal and visual interpretation, as well as imagination and sensitivity from both actors and audience.

Ford's use of the stage structure and its fittings is interesting in a period in which companies and playgoers alike were increasingly concerned with *how* things were done as against *what* was being done. Plays written for the Caroline private theatres are usually well supplied with stage directions containing frequent reference to the several doors, to upper and lower stage levels, to windows and hangings and to 'passing over the stage'. Of all this Ford's plays are particularly good examples and his precise instructions as to the use of lights on stage suggests that he regarded stage lighting as a matter of prime importance. Stage directions in themselves give a valuable insight into what was going on and what a dramatist might expect to happen.[4] A characteristic of Ford is his sensitivity to what carefully placed exits and entrances, and appearances above stage and behind withdrawn hangings, can do to underline the meaning or modify the tone of an episode. Throughout his mature independent work Ford seems to be increasingly stage conscious. He was also more alive than many of his contemporaries to what could be made of the intimacy of these small indoor theatres. Intimacy, the sense of an enclosure and then of a small interrelated community is a persistent characteristic; in fact the layout of the two theatres he worked in seems to have been so congenial to his way of thinking that it may, to some extent, have conditioned the planning of his later work.

How important the masque influence was to Ford is uncertain. We have no precise knowledge as to what scenery was available in the professional theatre or whether any of the more elaborate scenic effects of the masque were possible. Ford must have known of the quarrel, perhaps one of the most famous in theatrical history, between Ben Jonson and Inigo Jones as to the relative importance of the script and the staging in the masques at Court, where to Jonson's mind the extravagance of the decor not only distracted attention from the text but often mangled the author's intention. It was a problem of priorities which every producer knows! The problem was never resolved between Jonson and Jones and no doubt contributed a good deal to the former's disillusionment. Ford never missed an opportunity for a masque but such episodes are generally simply managed and call for little scenic background; they are moreover entirely functional to the requirements of the play. Simplicity combined with a thorough use of the stage was evidently a fundamental principle. Yet in Ford's plays crowdfull scenes are frequent, often opening with a flourish and some spectacle, and ending in a passage of dialogue to cover preparations for the next scene on the full stage. Swiftness and economy in scene-changing and clarity as to locality and purpose seem to have been his object.

Spectacle and pageantry were no doubt attractive to Ford for their own sake, as well as for their appeal to the audience, but the visual quality of the plays is evidence of something fundamental to his thinking. Ford seems to have conceived his character's mental and emotional processes in terms of visual figure — even a heart is physically described — so that they come to grips with their problems through patterns of behaviour or through the medium of striking emblematic devices. Masques and pageantry tend therefore to be less important to meaning than formal groupings or ritualistic and symbolic action. Hippolita's masque is a plot device, but Giovanni's final appearance with the impaled heart gathers up the central experience of the play. The same is true of the triptych of Orgilus, Ithocles and the dead Penthea, and to a lesser degree, of Calantha's dance. Similarly Stanley's marking of the informer's cheek with a cross stresses what is to be the first in a series of betrayals in *Perkin Warbeck*. Even when the setting is domestic as in *The Lady's Trial* the climactic scenes have a visual formality — a banquet or a mock court of justice.

The variation between the plays in the handling of figures and in general style is of immense interest; indeed the gulf between the lyricism of *The Lover's Melancholy* and the largely undecorated style of *The Lady's Trial* is startling. The musical movement of the verse in much of *The Lover's Melancholy*, the use of sustained and often arresting imagery — of the riven heart in *'Tis Pity* and *Love's Sacrifice*, of the crown and melting cloud shapes in *The Broken Heart*, of witchcraft and allied presentments of deception in *Perkin Warbeck* — recurring especially in the tragedies with the obsessiveness of images in dreams, the comparative absence of figure in the reasoned dialogue in the main plot of *The Lady's Trial*, are all dictated by the play's requirements. Yet as I have tried to show, in the same play can be found both that 'strength of feeling' in contrast to 'the quietness of the statement' to which Miss Bradbrook draws attention,[5] and the plain, unvarnished talk between one character and another — an unusual versatility within the self-imposed limits of a familiar but outdated dramatic pattern.

The same self-imposed limits may partly explain the lack, in three of the plays, of sufficient material to sustain five acts. In every play Ford had something important to say, a theme to develop and modify from older models, a well-used pattern to reshape, human motive in particular situations to analyse and explore. The selection such a task demanded he could meet with discernment, but he seems at times to have lacked the inventiveness either to bridge the gaps between key scenes or to harmonise the plot and its ancillary material into a whole. This is especially true of *Love's Sacrifice* and *The Lady's Trial*, while in *'Tis Pity* Ford's preoccupation with the iconoclastic aspect of incestuous love heightens the theme to a pitch of obsession. At the same time he had demonstrated that the older forms of drama were not necessarily outworn and that their revival might have a stimulating and disciplinary effect upon the fashionable theatre of his day. That he knew what he was about and that his intention was both realistic and worthwhile, the achievement of *The Broken Heart* is sufficient witness.

'Decadence' as applied to the work of so untiring an experimentalist as John Ford would seem a contradiction in terms. As Professor Anderson suggests of *'Tis Pity*, 'decadence ... depends largely upon the attitude of the reader.'[6] Those who confuse the values of Ford's characters with his own, instead of assessing them as part of the thematic pattern of the play, are bound to find a good deal of his work decadent. Nor could any responsible critic deny Ford's lapses in style and dramatic control. He was as capable of mixed metaphor, of clumsy handling of figure — and that in course of intensive dramatic action — as of brash horseplay in some of the comic relief in which he took refuge when material ran out. A good deal of this may result from that extreme selectiveness in order to concentrate upon a particular aspect of his theme which often led him into unjustifiable exaggeration, or concentration upon an immediate effect such as the rhythm of a song in which, as Miss Bradbrook notes, he was inclined to 'rock himself to sleep'.[7] But it will not do to take a passage out of its context as Mr Salingar does in citing Ithocles' complaint —

Death waits to waft me to the Stygian bank
And free me from this chaos of my bondage —
(III.2:p.229)

as an instance of a decadent attitude in that it is 'the mood of a man who has turned his back upon life'.[8] Ithocles is indeed voicing a death wish but it is precisely this attitude of mind that Penthea's function in the play is to probe and rebuke; the 'listless, nostalgic cadence' is a necessary adjunct to the dramatic development at this point.

Similarly Mr Tomlinson criticises the reconciliation scene between Annabella and Soranzo in *'Tis Pity* (IV.3) as ill-motivated and unconvincing[9] without considering its impact after Vasques' interruption of Soranzo's fury. Vasques' blunt, jog-trot prose is an interlude of calculated contrast; in the course of it, it is Vasques who now does the talking, the other two merely putting in a word here and there. The effect is derisive rather than ironic, but the intention is surely made perfectly clear in Vasques' aside — 'Sir, in any case smother your revenge.' When the verse resumes in a manner which Mr Tomlinson calls 'softly sentimental', Vasques is still there to jog the audience with more asides to Soranzo — 'Temper with some passion; be brief and moving; 'tis for a purpose', and Soranzo obeys — 'And wouldst thou use me thus — O Annabella.' Mr Tomlinson has obviously not noticed here a parody of the episode in which Frankford both rebukes and appeals to his erring wife in *A Woman Killed with Kindness* (IV.6). The scene in Heywood's play is both moving and sententious and its impact upon the contemporary theatre was no doubt considerable. Here is the dramatic irony 'which is in fact supposed to be taking place' and its effectiveness is thrust home when Annabella has left the stage, with Soranzo's line —

'I carry hell about me; all my blood is fired in swift revenge.' The whole episode is dominated by Vasques and seems designed rather to prepare for the part he is to play as an instrument of vengeance than to develop the character of his master.

Ford's failures are largely failures in judgement partly consequent upon lack of precedent for the combination of conservatism in form with experimentation in handling and content which was inherent in the task he had set himself. But whatever faults may be found in stylistic detail there is nothing hollow or effete about the overall conception and purpose of his plays. Ford never evades an issue, never foreshortens motive or character to tie up the ends of a plot. Nor does he surprise without preliminary warning or shock without a clearly discernible intention.

In middle age, with a good deal of professional experience behind him, Ford seems to 'take on' the Caroline theatre with a persistent determination to raise it to the level of its opportunities. He rejected compromise, he rejected empty idealism, offering instead a realism as ruthless as Middleton's combined with a sensitivity and, at his best, a quality of dramatic poetry often lacking on the contemporary stage. With Ford the Muses sang again and 'chattered' very little. He had neither rivals nor followers, for his ability to face both ways in theatrical development had no parallel. The logical follow-up to his work was in the Restoration theatre — the slight affinity with Dryden has already been commented upon — where notwithstanding its limitations tragedy became popular again, but the gulf between Elizabethan and Caroline drama was never to be bridged. Ford stands alone, his achievement modified in that in his own time he was inimitable.

We need to take a fresh look at Ford, to see his art whole and in its proper environment, the theatre. For rewarding as are the reading and study of the plays, it is in the theatre that their variety of pattern and style, even the peculiarities which may strike a reader as tedious or irrelevant, fall into place and justify their purpose. For they are dictated by the many facets of the intention which made him the kind of dramatist he was — the search for that harmony within the human spirit 'to whose sweet music All our actions dance'.

Appendix *The Queen* or *The Excellency of her Sex*

HISTORY OF THE PLAY

The Queen was published anonymously in 1653 and remained anonymous until 1906 when Professor W. Bang edited the play and attributed it to Ford. Sherman in 1908, H. Dugdale Sykes in 1924 and Joan Sargeaunt in 1935 were all in agreement.[1] More recently Professor H. J. Oliver in 1955 and Professor D.K. Anderson Jr. in 1972 both confirm Bang's opinion and most scholars would now attribute the play in its entirety to Ford.[2]

MAJOR THEMES

The theme underlying the main plot is the cure of misogyny by arousing jealous suspicions in order to stimulate sexual attraction. This therapeutic idea has been attributed to the influence of Burtonian psychology. The subject is Alphonso, sentenced to death for rebellion but pardoned and married to the Queen, whose sex, however, he abhors. The agent is his counsellor Muretto who, by dropping into his master's mind suspicions of the Queen's relations with the young lord Petruchi, rouses him to a fury of sexual jealousy.

Out of this theme three others develop. First is the trial of love, for the Queen endures with fortitude Alphonso's refusal to accept her as a wife and his subsequent accusation of unchastity. Second is the theme of honour; the Queen remains entirely loyal to her husband and also to her responsibilities towards her subjects, for she will allow none of them to risk life and limb by taking up the challenge of her cause. The theme of honour recurs in the secondary plot in Velasco's unwillingness to break the oath which he has sworn to the imperious Salassa even when she frees him from it. These typically Caroline ideas derive mainly from the romances and

161

might be calculated to appeal both to the popular and to the private theatre-goer.

Both the major and the minor plots build up the third theme — that of the stabilising effect of marriage on which the Queen comments —

> This sacred matrimonial tye of hearts
> Called marriage has Divinity within't.
>
> (II.1888)

EVIDENCE OF AUTHORSHIP

The case for Ford's authorship of *The Queen* has been based on textual parallels and similarities in theme and situation. Verbal similarities are always partly subjective and therefore liable to error, but Sykes' review of the findings of Bang and Sherman coupled with his own and followed by those of more recent scholars are convincing and I can add nothing of importance to them. Similarities to Ford's independent work in theme, situation and treatment seem to me of greater value. The trial of love is to be reckoned with in *Love's Sacrifice* and it is the major theme of *The Lady's Trial*. The closely associated idea of honour is the basic problem of *Love's Sacrifice*, *The Broken Heart* and *The Lady's Trial*, while the Queen's sense of the responsibilities of royal status is a preoccupation in *The Lover's Melancholy* and *Perkin Warbeck*. The importance of marriage as a means to stability, both in the individual and in the community, to a greater or lesser degree runs through Ford's independent plays.

But apart from these major themes a number of incidents are strongly reminiscent of Ford. The opening lines plunge us immediately into a challenging situation — 'All's free and all forgiven ... Bless her majesty!' — a curtain-raiser not dissimilar in effect from the opening of *Love's Sacrifice* and *'Tis Pity*. The following verbal combat between Muretto and the astrologer Pynto resembles the 'flyting' between Corax and Rhetias in *The Lover's Melancholy*. In his cunning handling of his master Muretto obviously recalls the practices of D'Avolos in *Love's Sacrifice*. Another possible parallel is with Iago's deception of Othello, but if the dramatist had

Shakespeare's play in mind he made very little use of it — surprising considering the dependence upon it of *Love's Sacrifice*. There is a hint of Desdemona — 'a child to chiding' — but more perhaps of 'patient Grissill' in the Queen's reaction after unsuccessfully pleading with her husband:

> what was't he said?
> That I no more should see him, never, never ...

> Not see him?
> 'twas too unkinde a task. But he commanded.
> (II.1255)

In fact this passage has touches — 'unkinde', 'no more should see him ... not see him' — of the authentic Ford. The attempt to exploit Velasco's weakness by inducing him to drink recalls the plight of Cassio, but the similarities with *Othello* are just enough to show that the dramatist was familiar with the play, but had not absorbed its theme and treatment to the point of reassessing them as had the Ford of *Love's Sacrifice*.

The use of a ring, the Queen's first gift to Alphonso, which he causes to be presented to Petruchi in her presence as a pledge of favour and her gay confiscation of it so that she may re-present it to Alphonso, slightly recall the episode of Calantha's ring in *The Broken Heart*.[3]

But in every case, whether in the development of a theme or in the handling of an episode, the superficial similarities merely demonstrate the play's inferiority. Beyond a brief exposition the dramatic opening leads nowhere for it is cut short by the quarrel which, in contrast to that between Corax and Rhetias, is without dramatic significance and degenerates into scurrility for its own sake; it is also prolonged to the point of tediousness. Whereas the ring episode in *The Broken Heart* is functional to the action and sparks off a new development in three main characters, the scene here is a piece of stage trickery designed to evoke a sentimental sympathy with the Queen when later disillusionment falls upon her. It is one of several examples in the play of writing for effect rather than meaning.

The debt to Burton in the main plot may be admitted, but in the generally flattened characterisation of this play psychological complexity is hardly possible. Alphonso is a

puppet going through the motions of psychological conflict
but passion never goes further with him than rhetoric or
childish truculence. 'I am not sorry', he replies to the Queen's
injunction to repentance for his late disloyalty, 'Nay nor will
not be sorry, know from me I hate your sex in general.' That
Muretto should reveal nothing of his purpose in asides or
soliloquy is typical of Ford, but as the play is constructed we
see so little of his plan in action and hear the truth so late in the
fifth act that his behaviour seems unnecessarily devious. When
he finally explains himself it is at an undramatic length in flat
prose. The main plot halts for lack of a clearly conceived
motivation.

Salassa and Velasco again go through the motions but
against Thamasta and Menaphon, with whom they have been
compared, they are little more than predictable exponents of
well-worn ideas. It is difficult to believe in the major
characters, and while Bufo's bawdry and Pynto's visions have
some life in them neither contributes anything to the dramatic
intention.

But whatever the play lacks in planning and motivation it
abounds in opportunities for the kind of spectacle a popular
audience would appreciate. The presentation of a public
execution with the added excitement of a last-minute reprieve
was likely to please and the dramatist is not niggardly! There
are three such scenes, following the same visual pattern, and
Salassa's entrance to execution with 'her hair loose' also
includes the victim's facile last maxims from the scaffold. The
fifth act with the summoning of the three champions and their
entrances in full armour — the stage directions are specific —
is a sustained pageant. This repetitiveness, without the
dramatic acceleration which Ford achieves in Meleander's
subtly varied reception of the Prince's gifts in *The Lover's
Melancholy*, is a surprising characteristic in a play attributed
to a dramatist whose economy in handling a main plot is a
feature of his authentic work.

A general flatness of tone and a falling short of purpose are
characteristic of this play. A useful contrast is that between
Alphonso's praise of the Queen's beauty and Giovanni's lines
addressed to Annabella in *'Tis Pity*.

I have surveyed the wonder of her cheeks,
Compared them with the lillies and the rose

And by my life Muretto, roses are
Adulterate to her blush and lillies pale
Examined with her white.

(*The Queen*, IV.2407)

These lines can mean no more than that the Queen's cheeks are
pinker than the rose and whiter than the lily. Compare with
the concentration of Giovanni's praise of Annabella:

The lily and the rose, most sweetly strange,
Upon your dimpled cheek do strive for change;
Such lips would tempt a saint; such hands as those
Would make an anchorite lascivious.

(*'Tis Pity*, I.3:p.109)

There follows on Alphonso's lines a passage in which the
author may have intended to give a hint of the dénouement by
suggesting an as yet unexplained irony in Muretto,
underlying Alphonso's newly-awakened love. If this was his
purpose he signally failed, for the dialogue rapidly
degenerates into something bordering on farce:

Alph. She is superlative. *Mur.* Divine. *Alph.* Rich, bright.
Mur. Immortal. *Alph.* Too, too worthy for a man.
Alph. The gods might enjoy her.

(IV.2437)

This is a failure in judgement as well as in dramatic control.

SUMMARY

Yet with all this there seems little doubt that *The Queen* is by
Ford and since it is of fairly even quality, probably by him in
its entirety. The parallels in theme and episode may be hollow
reflections of his authentic work, but they are still
characteristic and too numerous to be ignored. The play's
weaknesses suggest that it may be of an early date, a conclusion
slightly supported by the evidence of a no more than theatre-
goer's interest in *Othello* as against Ford's extensive
borrowings from that play in *Love's Sacrifice*. It is difficult to
believe that he would not have shown a deeper knowledge of

Othello had *The Queen* been written later than *Love's Sacrifice*. As has been shown, while motivation is not a strong point spectacle and sensationalism are dominant features. In fact the play seems designed to catch the interest not only of the private theatre but also that of the popular audience in one of the large open theatres such as the Globe.

There remains the question why the play should have been published anonymously. Although Ford's plays are difficult to date precisely it seems likely that they were all printed within a reasonable interval after performance. The dedications suggest that he took some interest in the publication of his work. The exceptional case of *The Queen* may be partly consequent on the play's remaining in repertory — evidence perhaps less of neglect than of its popularity.

Assuming that *The Queen* is early work, its interest for the student of Ford's independent plays is in its evidence that his major themes had been germinating in his mind from the outset of his career as a dramatist. Otherwise *The Queen* adds nothing to Ford's reputation and is misleading as an example of his art.

Notes

CHAPTER 1

1. Una Ellis-Fermor, *The Jacobean Drama*, p. 229.
2. Joan Sargeaunt, *John Ford*.
3. Una Ellis-Fermor, op. cit.
4. See M. C. Bradbrook, *Themes and Conventions of Elizabethan Tragedy*, pp. 250ff.; L. C. Salingar, 'The Decline of Tragedy' (*The Age of Shakespeare*) pp. 348 ff.; T. B. Tomlinson, *Elizabethan and Jacobean Tragedy*, pp. 266-74.
5. G. F. Sensabaugh, *The Tragic Muse of John Ford*; S. Blaine Ewing Jr., *Burtonian Melancholy in the Plays of John Ford*.
6. Mark Stavig, *John Ford and the Traditional Moral Order*; Irving Ribner, *Jacobean Tragedy*.
7. This is assuming that Ford's surviving Phoenix plays were written after 1625. F. E. Halliday notes that Queen Henrietta's Men were acting at the Phoenix between 1625 and 1637. The Lady Elizabeth's Men were at the same theatre for a short period from 1622 (*A Shakespeare Companion*, p. 57).
8. For a detailed examination of conditions in the Blackfriars Theatre see Glynne Wickham, *Early English Stages*, vol. 2 pt. II, pp. 123ff.
9. For the importance of this movement across the entire stage see 'Passing over the Stage' by Allardyce Nicoll, *Shakespeare Survey* no. 12, pp. 47-55.
10. Alfred Harbage, *Shakespeare and the Rival Traditions*, p. 43.
11. See Induction to *The Staple of News*, *Plays of Ben Jonson* (Everyman Edn., 1910) vol. II, p. 348:
    Bookholder (within).
    > Mend your lights gentlemen — Master prologue begin. (Enter tiremen to mend the lights.) These carry no firework to fright you but a torch in their hands.
12. Glynne Wickham, op. cit., pp. 83-4.
13. No plans or specifications of the reconstructions at the Phoenix theatre survive. These details are based partly on plans now in Worcester College, Oxford, for the rebuilding of a cockpit. Recent authorities believe these plans are those of Inigo Jones for the reconstruction of the Cockpit-in-Court. If Glynne Wickham is right in assuming that the King's Men had a good deal of influence on this conversion, these plans may well represent what most London companies and their audiences might expect of a private theatre. They offer, of course, a clue, not a solution, to the problem of the Phoenix. For details of the reconstructed Cockpit-in-Court see Glynne Wickham, op. cit., pp. 177ff.
14. See Alfred Harbage, op. cit., p. 45.
15. Induction to *The Magnetic Lady*, op. cit., vol. II, p. 506.

16. 'It is remarkable that, during a period soon to be denounced as the most oppressive and tyrannical England had ever endured, there are so few signs of widespread discontent, certainly none of organised resistance' (David W. Petegorsky, *Left Wing Democracy in the English Civil War*, p. 43).

17. David Matthew, *The Age of Charles I*, p. 195.

18. Petegorsky, op. cit., p. 35.

19. Clifford Leech, *Shakespearian Tragedy and other Studies in 17th Century Drama*, p. 161.

20. *The Antipodes* I. 2 (*Six Caroline Plays*, World's Classics, ed. A. S. Knowland, O.U.P., 1962, p. 267).

21. Donald K. Anderson Jr. has some interesting comments on the poem and its background (see *John Ford*, pp. 17-21).

22. See Donald K. Anderson Jr., op. cit., p. 23.

23. This is surmise, but since Webster and Massinger were both associated with the private theatres it seems a likely suggestion. The tone of the Prologue supports this view:

    A worthy story howsoever writ
    For Language, Modest Worth, Conciet or Wit
    Meets oftentimes with the sweet commendation
    Of 'hang't 'tis scurvy' when for approbation
    A jig shall be clap't at . . . Hither
    Come nobler judgments and to these the strain
    Of our invention is not bent in vain.

    (*The Works of John Webster*, ed. F. L. Lucas, London 1927, vol. IV, p. 158.) For a discussion of the authorship of this play see pp. 148-52.

24. In *The Witch of Edmonton* the Frank/Winnifred scenes and some passages between Frank and Susan are probably mainly by Ford, although it is unwise to assign any scene as a whole to a single author.
    H. Dugdale Sykes attributed *The Spanish Gipsy* as a whole to Ford (*Sidelights on Elizabethan Drama*, pp. 183-9). Others have found in it evidence of the work of Middleton and Rowley. I can find no clear indication of Middleton's hand, but Rowley may have had a good deal to do with the gipsy scenes. A number of passages in the action of the main plot, especially the Clara/Roderigo scenes, are in Ford's tragic manner.

25. The subject may have drawn from William Heminge, in his *Elegy on Randulpho's Finger*, the well-known lines —
    Deep in a dumpe Iacke Forde alone was gott
    With folded Armes and Melancholye hatt.

26. That the play was well received and that it was regarded as a promise for the future is suggested in a verse preface by William Singleton. It was, he says, 'by the best approved'; but 'As thou hast done enough thou canst do more.'

27. The precise order of the three tragedies published in 1633 is complicated by the fact that the King's Men, who acted *The Lover's Melancholy*, also presented *The Broken Heart*, whereas *'Tis Pity* and *Love's Sacrifice* were both acted at the Phoenix. Gerald Bentley believes that when Ford embarked on his independent work he wrote first for the King's Men and afterwards for the Beeston companies at the Phoenix (see *The Jacobean and Caroline Stage*, vol. III). It would therefore be logical to suppose, as Professor Oliver and Professor Anderson argue, that *The Broken Heart*

came immediately after *The Lover's Melancholy*. The position is slightly strengthened by a possible association between the main plot of *'Tis Pity* and the incestuous marriage of Sir Giles Allington and Dorothy Dalton, for which they were severely punished in 1631. The point is noted by Joan Sargeaunt and Professor Oliver. This would place *'Tis Pity* not earlier than 1631 and therefore probably last in the group.

While all this is interesting it is scarcely evidence. We must accept that Ford was a well-known Phoenix dramatist; the plays in which he collaborated and his three last plays, *Perkin Warbeck*, *The Fancies Chaste and Noble* and *The Lady's Trial*, were written for that theatre. Deliberate choice or professional circumstances, both beyond our guess, may explain why two of his most interesting plays should have found their way into the hands of the King's Men, the leading company in London. As I have shown in later chapters, certain passages in *Love's Sacrifice* have an immediate association with *'Tis Pity She's a Whore* and seem to be a matter of deliberate recall for dramatic effect, whereas parallels in *The Broken Heart* are less impressive and appear to be no more than echoes.

It cannot be denied that *'Tis Pity* dominates Ford's imagination during this period, but to a diminishing extent. I find it difficult to believe that *'Tis Pity* could have occurred anywhere but at the outset of his tragic phase.

28. There is some diagreement as to the date of the first performance of this play, although most authorities place it last in Ford's career. It must have been written between 1621, the date of Bacon's *History of the Reign of Henry the Seventh*, the principal source of Ford's material, and 1634, the date of its publication. The possibility that the conception of Henry VII as peacemaker was intended as a compliment to King James (see D. K. Anderson Jr., op. cit., p. 80) would date the play not later than 1625, the year of the King's death, and about three years before *The Lover's Melancholy*, with which, however, beyond its psychological interest it shows very little relationship. On the other hand affinities both in style and content with *The Broken Heart* (see Chapter 6) suggest that *Perkin Warbeck* is more logically placed in the period of that play and perhaps fairly soon after it. If *Perkin Warbeck* represents a return to the Beeston companies at the Phoenix, where Ford's two last plays were staged, it was probably written a little later than *The Broken Heart*, approximately 1633/4.

29. S. B. Ewing suggests an early date for *The Fancies* — before 1631/2, the date of Shirley's *Changes*, in which he believes Ford's play is ridiculed. See *Burtonian Melancholy in the plays of John Ford*, p. 28ff., also cited by D. K. Anderson Jr., op. cit., p. 119). The play was entered in the Stationers' Register with *The Lady's Trial* in 1638.

30. Op. cit., p. 261.

31. *The Problem of John Ford*, H. F. Oliver, p. 127.

CHAPTER 2

1. I believe this to be the meaning of the play, but of course the argument is fallacious. For the suffering in the symbolic forest could all have been

avoided had Bellario seen fit to reveal her sex earlier. But in that case there would have been no play!

2. Professor Stavig notes that the contest of Parthenophil and the nightingale suggests the art/nature conflict in which Parthenophil wins by the discipline of art (op. cit. pp. 76—7).

3. John Webster, who was certainly responsible for some of the best-known of the 'Characters' attributed to Sir Thomas Overbury in 1615, was masterly in his use of the 'character' form to introduce important figures in his own plays. A typical example is the introduction of the Duchess and her brothers in *The Duchess of Malfi*, acted at Blackfriars about 1617. In the same play the malcontent Bosola and the incompetent doctor are instances of the conventional stage types Ford seems to ridicule here.

4. An example is the parting scene in *The Duchess of Malfi* (III. 5). A still better but much earlier instance is the colloquy over Feliche's body in Marston's *Antonio's Revenge* (IV 5) written for the Children of Paul's, with whom music was much in demand.

5. See the well-known lines int the Prologue to *Antonio's Revenge*:
>   But if a breast
> Nail'd to the earth with griefe: if any heart
> Pierc't through with anguish, pant within this ring:
> If there be any blood whose heat is choakt
> And stifled with true sense of misery:
> If ought of these straines fill this consort up,
> Th'arrive most welcome.

(*The Plays of John Marston*, ed. Harvey Wood, *Blackfriars Dramatist*, (1934) pp. 69-70)

6. Op. cit., p. 129.

7. See 'The Discovery Space in Shakespeare's Globe', Richard Hosley, *Shakespeare Survey*, vol. 12, 1959, p. 45. Hosley believes that actors in Shakespeare's theatre were discovered by the use of hangings. He is, of course, referring to the Globe, but the same practice was probably followed at the company's other theatre at Blackfriars.

CHAPTER 3

1. See *'Tis Pity She's a Whore*, ed. Brian Morris (New Mermaid Edition), p. viii. Morris quotes on the matter S. P. Sherman's edition of the play, 1915.

2. *New Statesman*, 11 August 1972, pp. 103-4.

3. Professor Mark Stavig interprets the play as an exposure of the Platonic idea of equal love carried to excess and believes the final episode is entirely ironic. (Op. cit., *passim.*)

   Professor Irving Ribner believes the final statement of the play is that man must 'conform to a moral order whose inadequacy he always knows' so that the lovers are trapped between the demands of their own natures — their fate — and a world totally inadequate to their needs. (Op. cit., p. 163.)

   On the other hand Professor Donald K. Anderson Jr. notes that in estranging our sympathies from Soranzo Ford prepares for 'a remarkable variation on a familiar theme' in having an 'incestuous adulterer seek vengeance upon the cuckolded husband'. (Op. cit., pp. 100 and 103.)

4. Evidently the distasteful nature of the subject conditioned T. S. Eliot's surprising response to the play — 'it hardly rises above the purely carnal ... Giovanni is merely selfish and self-willed ... Annabella is pliant, vacillating and negative; the one almost a monster of egotism, the other virtually a moral defective'. (*Elizabethan Dramatic Essays* 1963, pp. 125-6.)

5. Professor Sensabaugh notes that 'more vigorously than in any of his plays Ford shows the strength of fate in *'Tis Pity She's a Whore*. (Op. cit., p. 156.)
   But to Irving Ribner Giovanni's acceptance of fate is an acknowledgment of 'his human condition with all its inevitable consequences'. (Op. cit., p. 166.)

6. Surprisingly, Clifford Leech refers to Bergetto's 'absurd death'. (Op. cit., p. 63.)

7. Professor Sensabaugh sees the fate motive as Giovanni's excuse for prurient passion. He comments — 'Fate as an excuse to follow individual whim could hardly go beyond this.' (Op. cit., pp. 156-7.)

8. This was evidently the interpretation of the Friar's role in the National Theatre production of August 1972. In the review quoted above Benedict Nightingale refers to Annabella as 'the numb terrified puppet of an unusually powerful and intense priest'.

9. See *Doctor Faustus*, Everyman Edition (1909) p. 157: 'You stars that reigned at my nativity'.

10. Op. cit., p. 117.

11. *The Duchess of Malfi* (V.5.2.) ed. F. L. Lucas, *Works of John Webster*. Vol. II.

12. *Duchess of Malfi*, IV.2.20 (ed. F. L. Lucas, 1927, Vol. II). (Spelling modernised.)
    Duchess. Dost thou think we shall know one another,
    　　　　In th'other world?
    　　　　Cariola. Yes out of question.

13. Brian Morris describes the heart and dagger as 'the perfect, final, visual image for what has been going on privately, secretly in their midst' (ed. Brian Morris, New Mermaid, p. xxiii).
    He is referring to the love between brother and sister and their joint vow, 'Love me or kill me'. 'The final spectacle is the fulfilment of the prophecy.' But as the vow was a private one, does not this interpretation make the public presentation of the visual image unnecessary?

14. Op. cit., pp. xxiv-xxvi.

CHAPTER 4

1. Typical parallels with *'Tis Pity* are:
   I.2: 'My heart entombed in yonder goodly shrine' — cf. *'Tis Pity*, IV. 3: 'in this piece of flesh ... had I laid up The treasure of my heart'; *'Tis Pity*, v. 6: 'A heart, my lords, in which is mine entombed.'
   II. 3: 'If when I am dead you rip This coffin of my heart ...' (repeated II. 4) — cf. *'Tis Pity*, v. 6: 'These hands have from her bosom ripped her heart.'

v. 3: 'Now come I to lay tribute to those wounds Which I digged up' — cf. *'Tis Pity*, v. 6: 'I digged for food in a much richer mine.'
The following passages from *Love's Sacrifice* are based on the same idea:
  IV. 1:   'I would unrip
       That womb of bloody mischief with these nails
       Where such a cursed plot as this was hatched.'
  IV. 2:   If you did stab me to the heart ...
                The heart,
       Nay strumpet to the soul and tear it off
       From life.'

2. See *Othello*, v. 2. 300.
3. Another parallel worth noting is with the plot of Heywood's domestic tragedy *The English Traveller*, in which the husband's friend Geraldine resists his love for the wife, but is maligned by the destroyer Delavil who seduces her himself.

    Both the anagrammatic name and the dramatic function of Delavil may have given Ford a hint for the conception of D'Avolos. The echo of *Othello* III. 3 in Delavil's play on 'honest' in the scene in which he arouses Old Geraldine's suspicions against his son (English Traveller, III. 1) is also worth noting.

4. See *The White Devil*, I. 1.ff.: 'Banisht! ... Courtly reward and punishment. Fortune's a right whore.'

    Ford may have had Lodovico the avenger in mind when considering Rosseilli's part in the action.

5. Mauruccio's imaginary portrait may slightly strengthen the argument for placing *Love's Sacrifice* fairly soon after *'Tis Pity She's a Whore*.
6. Professor Stavig has some interesting comments on the symbolic use in this play of the games of chess and maw (op. cit., pp. 130-1).
7. See v. 1: pp. 359-60, where a number of lines are lost or partially obliterated.
8. Peter Ure finds an explanation for Bianca's visit to Fernando's chamber in her implicit faith in his loyalty to an ideal love and the consequent safety of her honour with him. 'The wantonness of Bianca and the purity of Fernando are set against the background of the Platonic cult' — a cult to which Bianca is a failed initiate whereas Fernando is true to his ideal ('Cult and Initiates in Ford's *Love's Sacrifice*', p. 305).

    No doubt Ford had all this in mind, but he does not state it here in the definite terms to which Giovanni has recourse in defending his position to the Friar. Ford's attitude to Platonism is always objective and his use of its terminology generally reticent. In the interpretation of his plays it is perhaps safer to follow his lead.

9. For instance *The Changeling*, III. 4, in which De Flores reveals to Beatrice the nature and consequences of their joint act in the murder of Alonso for which she has commissioned him, or *Women Beware Women*, II. 1, where Livia unfolds to Isabella the fictitious story of her birth which leads her into incest. In either case the emphasis is on the mental suffering of the listener.
10. This is not the view of Professor Stavig, who sees the ending of the play as 'a serious analysis of the effects of passion' (op. cit., p. 136) and

believes that Ford's work in general is inspired by a quest for a moral order.

11. Op. cit., p. 14.

12. T. J. King notes the demands which *Love's Sacrifice* makes upon the staging at the Phoenix theatre. He also believes that a movable booth with curtains was used for the discovery scenes ('The Staging of Plays at the Phoenix in Drury Lane, 1616-42', *Theatre Notebook*, XIX, pp. 146-66.)

13. There are two outstanding examples in Marston's *Antonio's Revenge* — the discovery of Feliche's body hanging in a window, when the curtains are drawn back (I. 3) and the appearance of Andrugio's ghost 'betwixt the music houses' (v. 5). The play was first performed by the Children of Paul's, in 1601-2.

14. Hosley suggests that this may have been the practice at the Swan Theatre (op. cit., p. 43).

15. Miss Joan Sargeaunt, whose assessment of Ford is generally fair, is seriously concerned at what she sees as his failure in secondary material. He 'was not well qualified as a writer of melodrama and totally un-equipped and inefficient as a writer of low comedy. Ford seems to have believed it necessary to introduce one or both these elements into his tragedies and tragi-comedies' (op. cit., p. 70).

The case is however considerably weakened by Miss Sargeaunt's admission that even in the sub-plots Ford seems to have been successful in the theatre.

16. The impression of deliberate parody is strengthened by certain verbal echoes: Giovanni's triumph in his final act — 'the glory of my deed Darkened the mid-day sun' (*'Tis Pity*, v. 6: p. 177) — is reduced to the exultation of Ferentes' murderers — 'nor do we blush To call the glory of this murder outs' (III. 4: p. 343).

The sense of power in Giovanni's claim — 'In my fists I hold the twists of life' (*'Tis Pity*, ibid.) — becomes an expression of mere vindictiveness in the Duke's threat to Bianca — 'I am [awake]; and in my hand hold up The edge that must uncut thy twist of life.'

CHAPTER 5

1. Professor D. K. Anderson Jr. assigns *The Broken Heart* to a date close to that of *The Lover's Melancholy*, believing that the two plays were probably written in sequence since both were for the King's Men. Logically this may be a reasonable conclusion, but the gulf between the two plays in style and management of character and motive suggests that other work must have intervened. (See note 27 to Chapter 1.)

2. George Steiner, *The Death of Tragedy* (Faber, 1961) p. 7. See also Helen Gardner, *Religion and Literature* (Faber, 1971).

3. Op. cit., p. 67.

4. Brian Morris takes these lines as a statement of 'the moral norm of the play'. (*The Broken Heart*, New Mermaid edition, p. xv.)

5. Clifford Leech lays a good deal of emphasis on the role of Penthea (see note 7 below). No doubt many of Ford's contemporaries saw the play as

centring upon her, as for example in Crashaw's famous couplet —
  Thou cheat'st us Ford, make one seen two by art,
  What is Love's Sacrifice but the Broken Heart? —
where the play is obviously interpreted as a study of what happens when true lovers are sundered by a forced marriage.

6. Op. cit., p. 154.

7. Peter Ure finds some relevance to Penthea's position in that of the heroines of Heywood's two domestic dramas, *A Woman Killed with Kindness* and *The English Traveller*. Mrs Frankford of the first play starves to death, Mrs Wincott of the second dies, under the burden of remorse for marital disloyalty. In the context of Heywood's tragedies he notes that enforced or unsuitable marriages were much censured at the time of Ford's play. Ford's originality lies in that Penthea dies for the betrayal, not of a husband but of a 'legally contracted lover'. He thus 'cleverly combines the theme of the false wife stricken by conscience . . . and the theme of enforced marriage' ('Marriage and the Domestic Drama in Heywood and Ford', p. 215).

   These are topical associations which a contemporary audience would not be slow to understand, as is borne out in Crashaw's evident view — albeit a late one — in the couplet quoted in note 5 above, that Penthea's tragedy is the centre of the play.

8. *John Ford* (Writers and their Work) pp. 26-7. Penthea is here described as making Orgilus 'her instrument', this couplet being a forecast of the mad scene where Professor Leech believes Penthea incites Orgilus to vengeance.

   On the other hand Joan Sargeaunt notes a charity in Penthea's behaviour towards Ithocles — 'something beyond love and forgiveness' (op. cit., p. 83).

9. Professor D. K. Anderson Jr. notes that 'a major shift in plot occurs after Act I' and that Prophilus after the first act 'becomes a very minor character. Orgilus eventually destroys a marriage but it is that of ithocles and Calantha' (op. cit., p. 73).

10. Op. cit., p. 159. Ribner also stresses the importance of the 'engine' in the chair, which closes upon Ithocles with an irony which he finds 'crucial to the meaning of the play'.

11. Professor Stavig comments upon Ford's 'emblematic method' (op. cit., p. 144).

12. Clifford Leech believes that the fate references are part of a resignation demanded of all the characters in the play (*John Ford and the Drama of his Time*, p. 87).

13. *Form and Meaning in Drama*, p. 225.

14. *The Broken Heart*, New Mermaid edition, pp. xxviii-xxix.

15. There is a corruption in the text at this point. The last two-and-a-half lines are from Brian Morris' edition, and are taken from Smeaton's emendation of Gifford's text. (See Brian Morris, op. cit., notes, p. 92.)

16. There is of course nothing new in this device. Most of the full-stage scenes in Shakespeare's plays conclude in this manner. Apart from its artistic usefulness — a change of tone, a slackening of tension — it may well have proved of practical value in the Elizabethan theatre. Its importance here is in the emphasis its recurrent use throws upon the convenience of hangings across the entire stage.

CHAPTER 6

1. 'History of the Reign of King Henry the Seventh', in *Moral and Historical Works of Bacon*, Bohn edition, London 1857, p. 386.
2. Bacon, op. cit., p. 390; Gainsford, *True and Wonderful History of Perkin Warbeck*, Harleian Miscellany, 1808-13, pp. 513, 515.

    Warbeck's speech before the Scottish Court at his first appearance and that of James IV in which he excuses his dismissal of Warbeck later are produce sons in her old age, already tall striplings at that (I. 1: p. 385) — reaction to the defection of Stanley seems to derive from Gainsford (p. 522). Again the exchanges between King James and Warbeck at Norham Castle are clearly based upon Gainsford. In both the word 'dolent' appears and in both James suggests doubts of Warbeck's reliability considering the slenderness of his following — 'Duke of York, for such thous sayst thou art' — (III. 4: p. 434): compare Gainsford — 'your realm of which you say you are the undoubted heir' (p. 532).

    Ford repeats from Bacon the joke about the Lady Margaret's ability to produce sons in her old age, already tall striplings at that (I. 1: p. 385) — cf. Bacon p. 397 — and Bacon's description of Warbeck as a 'landloper' is repeated in Lambert Simnel's taunt (v. 3: p. 464). It is clear that Ford made the greater use of Bacon, but he was obviously familiar with Gainsford's account. It is possible of course that Bacon was also using Gainsford.

    Other suggested influences are from Shakespeare's *Richard II* and *Richard III*.
3. Op. cit., p. 391.
4. See Jonas A. Barish *'Perkin Warbeck* as Anti-History'. Barish believes Ford's intention is to present Warbeck as the rightful claimant. On the other hand Professor Donald K. Anderson Jr. suggests that Ford's 'idealised portrayal of Henry VII as a peacemaker seeks to praise James I' (op. cit., p. 80). See also D. K. Anderson Jr., 'Kingship in Ford's *Perkin Warbeck*', *ELH* (September 1960).
5. See Lawrence Babb, 'Abnormal Psychology in John Ford's *Perkin Warbeck*', where the influence of Burtoni and psychology is traced in the presentation of the central figure.
6. See 'The Mystery of *Perkin Warbeck*'.
7. In the production of *Perkin Warbeck* at 'The Other Place', Stratford-on-Avon, during the summer of 1975 Lady Katherine was presented as an enforced bride. Considering the play's deliberate ambiguity this interpretation, which aroused a good deal of criticism, was not wholly unjustifiable.
8. Op. cit., p. 82.

CHAPTER 7

1. See F. S. Boas, *Thomas Heywood* (1950) p. 44.
2. See note 3 to Chapter 4 above.
3. Ferdinando's sudden appearance in Bianca's tomb, dressed for his own burial, in the finale of *Love's Sacrifice* is no exception, for in the mutilated passage (v. 1: p. 360.) Ferdinando seems to reiterate his

intention that if she dies her sepulchre shall 'incoffin' him alive (see chapter 4).

4. Thomas Middleton, *Women Beware Women*, IV. 3 (Mermaid edition, 1887, p. 356).

5. 'Incked' may mean 'blotted out', or as Gifford suggests, the word may read 'nicked', suggesting a setback. Both interpretations carry the idea of reversal.

6. The parallel is with Winnifred's grief on hearing, Susan, whom her own husband Frank Thorney has married bigamously, refer to him as 'my husband':

   Oh gods! oh mine eyes! . . .
   Something hit mine eye — it makes it water still.
   (III. 2: Mermaid edition, p. 341).

7. Op. cit., p. 127.

8. It also recalls from *The Fancies* Flavia's unwisdom in her association with Camillo and Vespucci, and the evil pressure of 'opinion'.

9. *A Fair Quarrel* was written in collaboration with Rowley, but the duel scene, (III. 1) bears signs of Middleton's hand and can be attributed to him with some certainty.

10. See p. 134 above.

11. Typical examples are John Suckling's *Aglaura* and William Cartwright's *The Lady Errant*.

12. See *The Duchess of Malfi* (III. 5.2) where the Duchess complains: 'Is all our train Shrunk to this poor remainder?'

13. The Prologue continues:

    He who will venture on a jest, that can
    Rail on another's pain, or idly scan
    Affairs of state, oh he's the only man.

   The Prologue is thought to be by Theophilus Bird, an actor at the Phoenix who probably played a part in *The Lady's Trial*.

CHAPTER 8

1. Op. cit., p. 188.

2. Una Ellis-Fermor, op. cit., p. 245.

3. Op. cit., p. 75. Miss Sargeaunt attributes the failure of the Amoretta plot in *The Lady's Trial* to this deficiency. To me this secondary plot has its comic moments, but its partial failure may be explained by the dramatist's only half-engaged interest. Scenes of sustained bombast are not in Ford's line; we are apt to forget that he was the servant of his theatre!

4. An amusing instance occurs in the oyster scene in Killigrew's *The Parson's Wedding* (II. 7). There is a good deal of reference to oysters and the stage directions require 'A table and knives ready for oysters', but the oysters do not appear until more than half-way through the scene. At an intermediate point the widow says — 'Come shall we eat oysters?', but calls not for oysters but for wine, and a line or two later there is a direction — 'Oysters not brought in yet'. The real cue is the widow's later

order — 'Who's there? Bring in the oysters.' The scene is acted on the upper stage and this fact and the repetition in the dialogue had obviously caused confusion in the tiring house. (Op. cit., p. 478.)

5. Op. cit., p. 251.
6. Op. cit., p. 95.
7. Op. cit., p. 259.
8. L. G. Salingar, 'The Decline of Tragedy', *The Age of Shakespeare* (Pelican) p. 439.
9. Op. cit., p. 267.

APPENDIX

1. Stuart P. Sherman, 'A New Play by John Ford', *Modern Language Notes*, XXIII (December 1908); H. Dugdale Sykes, *Sidelights on Elizabethan Drama*, ch. VIII; Joan Sargeaunt, *John Ford*, Appendix 1.
2. H. J. Oliver, *The Problem of John Ford*; D. K. Anderson Jr., *John Ford*.
3. Some of the instances referred to above have been noted elsewhere. See D. K. Anderson, op. cit., pp. 43-4.

Select Bibliography

1. WORKS OF JOHN FORD

(a) *General editions*
Dyce, Alexander, and William Gifford, *The Works of John Ford*, three vols (1869 and 1895).
Ellis, H. Havelock, *John Ford* [five plays], Mermaid series (1888).
Gifford, William, *The Dramatic Works of John Ford*, two vols (1827).
Weber, Henry, *The Dramatic Works of John Ford*, two vols (Edinburgh, 1811).

(b) *Single plays*
'Tis Pity She's a Whore
Bawcutt, N. W., Regents Renaissance Drama Series (1966).
Morris, Brian, New Mermaid series (1968).

The Broken Heart
Anderson, Donald K., Jr., Regents Renaissance Drama Series (1968).
Morris, Brian, New Mermaid series (1966).
Smeaton, Oliphant, The Temple Dramatists (1906).

Perkin Warbeck
Anderson, Donald K., Jr., Regents Renaissance Drama Series (1965).
Struble, Mildred C. (University of Nebraska Press, 1926).
Ure, Peter, Revels Plays Series (1968).

The Queen
Bang, W., *Materialen* (Louvain, 1906).

2. RELEVANT STUDIES

(a) *Books*
Anderson, Donald K. Jr., *John Ford*, Twaynes English Authors series (Indiana University Press, 1972).
Bentley, Gerald E., *The Jacobean and Caroline Stage* (Clarendon Press, 1941-56).
Bowle, John, *Charles I* (Weidenfeld & Nicolson, 1975).
Bradbrook, M. C., *Themes and Conventions of Elizabethan Tragedy* (Cambridge University Press, 1935).
——— *The Living Monument, Shakespeare and the Theatre of his Time* (Cambridge University Press, 1975).
Davril, Robert, *Le Drame de John Ford* (Paris: Librairie Marcel Didier, 1954).
Ellis-Fermor, Una, *The Jacobean Drama* (Methuen, 1936).
Eliot, T. S., *Elizabethan Essays* (Faber, 1934).
Ewing, S. Blain Jr., *Burtonian Melancholy in the Plays of John Ford* (Princeton, 1940).
Gardner, Helen, *Religion and Literature* (Faber, 1971).

Halliday, F. E., *A Shakespeare Companion, 1564-1964* (Penguin, 1964).
Kitto, H. D. F., *Form and Meaning in Drama* (Methuen, 1956).
Lamb, Charles, *Specimens of the English Dramatic Poets* (Bell, 1890).
Leech, Clifford, *John Ford and the Drama of his Time* (Chatto & Windus, 1957).
―――― *John Ford*, Writers and their Work, No. 170 (Longman, 1964).
Matthew, David, *The Age of Charles I* (Eyre & Spottiswoode, 1951).
Nicoll, Allardyce, *The Development of the Theatre* (Harrap, 1927).
Oliver, Harold J., *The Problem of John Ford* (Melbourne University Press, 1955).
Ornstein, Robert, *The Moral Vision of Jacobean Tragedy* (University of Wisconsin Press, 1960).
Petegorsky, David W., *Left Wing Democracy in the English Civil War* (Gollancz, 1940).
Ribner, Irving, *Jacobean Tragedy* (Methuen, 1962).
Sargeaunt, M. Joan, *John Ford* (Blackwell, 1935).
Sensabaugh, George F., *The Tragic Muse of John Ford* (Stanford University Press, 1944).
Stavig, Mark, *John Ford and the Traditional Moral Order* (University of Wisconsin Press, 1968).
Steiner, George, *The Death of Tragedy* (Faber, 1961).
Sykes, H. Dugdale, *Sidelights on Elizabethan Drama* (Oxford University Press, 1924).
Tomlinson, T. B., *A study of Elizabethan and Jacobean Tragedy* (Oxford University Press, 1964).
Wickham, Glynne, *Early English Stages*, vols I and II (Routledge & Kegan Paul, 1959, 1963).

(b) *Articles and chapters of books*
Anderson, Donald K., Jr., 'The Heart and the Banquet Imagery in Ford's *'Tis Pity* and *The Broken Heart*', *Studies in English Literature*, II (spring 1962) pp. 209-17.
Babb, Lawrence, 'Abnormal Psychology in Ford's *Perkin Warbeck*', *Modern Language Notes*, LI (1936) pp. 234-37.
Barish, Jonas A., '*Perkin Warbeck* as Anti-History', *Essays in Criticism*, XX (1970) pp. 151-71.
Blayney, Glenn H., 'Convention, Plot and Structure in *The Broken Heart*', *Modern Philology*, LVI (August 1958) pp. 1-9.
Harbage, Alfred, 'The Mystery of *Perkin Warbeck*', in *Studies in the English Renaissance Drama* (Peter Owen and Vision Press, 1959) pp. 125-41.
Hosley, Richard, 'The Discovery Space in Shakespeare's Globe', in *Shakespeare Survey No. 12* (1959) pp. 35-46.
Kaufman, R. J., 'Ford's Tragic Perspective', *Texas Studies in Literature and Language*, I (winter 1960) pp. 522-37.
King, T. J., 'Staging of Plays at the Phoenix Theatre in Drury Lane, 1617-42', *Theatre Notebook*, XIX (spring 1965).
Knight, G. Wilson, 'John Ford Dramatist of the Heart', Devonshire Association for the Advancement of Science, Literature and Art, *Report and Transactions*, vol. 103, 1971.

Nicoll, Allardyce, 'Passing Over the Stage', in *Shakespeare Survey No. 12*
(1959) pp. 47-55.

Ure, Peter, 'Cult and Initiates in Ford's *Love Sacrifice*', *Modern Language
Quarterly*, xi (September 1950) pp. 298-306.

—— 'Marriage and the Domestic Drama in Heywood and Ford', English
Studies, xxxi (October 1951) pp. 200-16.

Salingar, L. G., 'The Decline of Tragedy', in *The Age of Shakespeare*
(Penguin edition, 1955) pp. 429-30.

Index

Agamemnon, The, 80-3, 96; *see also*
  Oresteia
Aglaura, 8, 176n.11; *see also*
  Suckling
All for Love, 154; *see also* Dryden
Allington, Sir Giles, 37, 169n.27
Anatomy of Melancholy, The, 7, 16;
  see also Burton
Anderson, Donald, K. Jr., 123, 158,
  161, 168nn.21,22, 169nn.28,29,
  170n.3, 173n.1, 174n.9, 175n.4,
  177n.23
An Ill Beginning has a Good End, 9
Antipodes, The, 8, 168n.20; *see also*
  Brome
Antonio's Revenge, 37, 170nn.3,5,
  173n.13; *see also* Marston
Athena, 97

Babb, Lawrence, 175n.5
Bacon, Francis, 106, 107, 109, 110,
  111, 122, 169n.28, 175n.2
Bang, W., 161
Barish, Jonas, A., 175n.4
Beaumont and Fletcher, 2, 10, 16, 19,
  28, 72, 90, 139
Beauty in a Trance, 9
Beeston, Christopher, 2, 4
  Beeston companies, 168n.27,
  169n.28
Bentley, Gerald, 168n.27
Bird, Theophilus, 8, 176n.13
Blackfriars Theatre, 2, 3-4, 5, 10, 11,
  12, 13, 16, 17, 27, 79, 102, 149,
  154, 167n.8, 170n.3
Boas, F. S., 175n.1
Bradbrook, M. C., 12, 158, 159,
  167n.4
Bristowe, Merchant, The, 10
Broken Heart, The, 8, 12, 14, 27, 30,
  42, 59, 72, 75, 78, 79-104, 105,
  117, 121, 122, 123, 124, 126, 144,
  152, 154, 155, 157, 158, 162, 163,

  168n.27, 169n.28, 173nn.1,4,
  174n.14
Brome, Richard, 8, 13, 58, 151, 154
Burton, Robert, 7, 11, 18, 104, 155,
  163

Caroline, 1, 2, 6, 12, 14, 58, 70, 105,
  106, 123, 125, 155, 161
Caroline Theatre, The, 1, 6, 14, 22,
  36, 58, 70, 99, 131, 144, 149, 150,
  151, 152
  Audience, 4-6, 7, 9, 16, 23, 56, 79,
  153
  Drama, 56, 151, 160
  Dramatists, 73, 141
  Stage, 1, 147, 151, 156
  Tragedy, 83
Cartwright, William, 6, 8, 23, 150,
  154, 176n.1
Cassandra/Tiresias, 81
Changeling, The, 76, 172n.9; *see*
  also Middleton
Chapman, George, 150, 151
Charles I, King, 1, 3, 4, 6, 150
Chekhovian, 71
Classical
  Dramatists, 98
  Tragedy, 79-80, 83, 104
  Tragic chorus, 95
Clytemnestra, 80, 82
Cockpit, The, 9: *see also* Phoenix
Cockpit-in-Court, The, 3, 4, 150
Commos, 27, 86
Corneille, Pierre, 15
Crashaw, Richard, 173n.5, 174n.7

Davenant, William, 4, 13, 151
Dekker, Thomas, 10, 12, 117-18, 132,
  155
Don Sebastian, 154; *see also* Dryden
Dryden, John, 154, 160
Duchess of Malfi, The, 38, 50-1, 55,

64, 170n.3, 171nn.11,12,
    176n.12; *see also* Webster
Duke of Milan, The, 59-62, 76; *see
    also* Massinger
D'Urfé, 10

Eliot, T. S., 171n.4
Elizabeth, Queen, 150
Elizabethan
    Drama, 151, 160
    Historical drama, 124
    Stage, 153
    Tragedy, 79-80, 98, 104, 152
Ellis-Fermor, Una, 1, 167nn.1,3,
    176n.2
English Traveller, The, 125, 126,
    172n.3, 174n.7; *see also*
    Heywood
Eumenides, The, 82
Evans, Henry, 2
Ewing, S. Blaine Jr., 167n.5, 169n.29

Fair Maid at the Inn, A, 11
Fair Quarrel, A, 140, 176n.9; *see also*
    Middleton
Fairy Knight, The, 10
Fame's Memorial, 9
Fancies Chaste and Noble, The, 12,
    38, 125, 126-34, 169nn.27,29,
    176n.8
Faustus, Doctor, 18; *see also*
    Marlowe
Fletcher, John, 141; *see also*
    Beaumont and Fletcher
Ford, John, 7, 8-9, 10, 14-15, 20, 23,
    35, 55-6, 152-3
Fortune Theatre, The, 4

Gainsford, Thomas, 106, 111,
    175n.2
Gardner, Helen, 173n.2
Gifford, William, 174n.15, 176n.5
Globe Theatre, The, 2, 3, 4, 10, 166

Halliday, F. E., 167n.7
Hamlet, 76
Harbage, Alfred, 3, 117, 167nn.10,14
Heminge, William, 168n.25
Henrietta Maria, Queen, 6, 7, 150,
    151

Henry, Prince, 150
Henry IV I, 108
Henry IV II, 122
Henry VII, History of the Reign of,
    106, 175n.1; *see also* Bacon
Heywood, Thomas, 12, 125, 126,
    136, 137, 143, 150, 151, 159,
    172n.3, 174n.7
Honest Whore, The, 117, 125, 127;
    see also Dekker
Honour Triumphant, 9
Hopkins, Gerard M., 101
Hosley, Richard, 173n.14

Inn of Court, 8

Jacobean, 1, 2, 12, 58, 72, 104
Jacobean Theatre, the, 5, 6
    Audience, 95
    Drama, 139
    Dramatists, 152
    Stage, 32, 153
    Tragedy, 24, 38, 78, 83
James I, King, 150, 169n.28, 175n.4
Jones, Inigo, 3, 6, 149, 156
Jonson, Ben, 4, 5, 13, 23, 125, 131,
    150, 151, 152, 156

Keep the Widow Waking, 11
King, T. J., 173n.12
King and No King, A, 51; *see also*
    Beaumont and Fletcher
King Lear, 16, 32, 76
King's Men, The, 2, 10, 167n.13,
    168n.27, 173n.1
Killigrew, Thomas, 8, 176n.4
Kitto, H. D. F., 98

Lady Errant, The, 176n.11; *see also*
    Cartwright
Lady's Trial, The, 8, 12, 14, 90, 125,
    126, 134-49, 153, 154, 155, 157,
    158, 162, 169n.28, 176nn.13,3
Lamb, Charles, 1
*Late Murder of the Son Upon the
    Mother, The*, 11
Laud, Archbishop, 6
Leech, Clifford, 7, 91, 168n.19,
    171n.6, 173n.5, 174nn.8,12
London Merchant, The, 9

Lover's Melancholy, The, 5, 11, 14, 16-35, 36, 44, 59, 86, 100, 125, 126, 153, 154, 157, 162, 164, 168n.27, 173n.1

Love's Sacrifice, 12, 58-78, 83, 97, 126, 139, 154, 157, 158, 162, 163, 165, 166, 168n.27, 172nn.1,5,8, 173n.12, 175n.3

Lucas, F. L., 171nn.11,12

Magnetic Lady, The, 23, 151, 167n.15; *see also* Jonson

Maid's Tragedy, The, 72, 140; *see also* Beaumont and Fletcher

Marlowe, Christopher, 18, 47

Marston, John, 30, 75, 151, 170n.4, 173n.13

Masque, The, 4, 6, 8, 18, 23, 26, 34, 41, 56, 58, 67
  Influence of, 156-7

Massinger, Philip, 7, 13, 58, 59, 62, 71, 151, 168nn.2,3

Matthew, David, 168n.17

Middleton, Thomas, 38, 54, 73, 78, 128, 140, 152, 160, 168n.24, 176nn.4,9

Morris, Brian, 99, 170nn.1,13, 174n.15

Mountjoy, Lord, 9

New Way to Pay Old Debts, A, 151; *see also* Massinger

Nicoll, Allardyce, 167n.9

Nightingale, Benedict, 38, 171n.8

Oliver, H. F., 12, 161, 169nn.27,3, 177n.2

Oresteia, The, 80, 83, 104

Othello, 12, 59-62, 67-72 *passim*, 76, 77, 163, 165, 166, 172nn.2,3

Other Place, The, 175n.7

Overbury, Sir Thomas, 170n.3

Parliament, 6

Parson's Wedding, The, 176n.4; *see also* Killigrew

Paul's, Children of, 170n.4, 173n.13

Pericles, 28

Perkin Warbeck, 9, 12, 14, 36, 105-24, 144, 148, 153, 154, 155, 157, 162, 175n.7, 169nn.27,28

Petergorsky, David W., 6, 168nn.16,18

Philaster, 16-17, 18, 21, 23, 26; *see also* Beaumont and Fletcher

Phoenix Theatre, The, 2, 3-4, 10, 11, 12, 13, 27, 35, 56, 58, 75, 105, 149, 154, 167n.7, 168n.27, 173n.12, 176n.13

Platonic, 7, 23, 28, 44, 73, 79, 172n.8
  Neo-Platonism, 26, 32, 49, 154

Queen, The, 9-10, 160-6

Queen and the Concubine, The, 151; *see also* Brome

Queen Anne's Men, 9

Queen Elizabeth's Men, 167n.7

Queen Henrietta's Men, 2, 18, 167n.7

Queen's Exchange, The, 151; *see also* Brome

Racine, Jean, 15

Restoration Theatre, the, 124, 149, 160

Reubens, 6

Revenger's Tragedy, The, 37, 126, 128, 129, 130, 131

Revenge Tragedy, 79
  Motive, 104
  Pattern of, 55, 153

Ribner, Irving, 96, 167n.6, 170n.3, 171n.5, 174n.10

Rich, Lord, 9; *see also* Mountjoy

Richard II, 113, 175n.2

Richard III, 175n.2

Roman Actor, The, 151; *see also* Massinger

Romeo and Juliet, 37, 43

Rowley, William, 10, 168n.24, 176n.9

Royal Combat, The, 9

Royal Slave, The, 8; *see also* Cartwright

Salingar, L. C., 159, 167n.4, 177n.8

Salisbury Court Theatre, 3

Sargeaunt, Joan, 1, 31, 83, 155, 161,

167n.2, 169n.27, 173n.15,
174n.8, 176n.3, 177n.1
Sensabaugh, G. F., 167n.5,
171nn.5,7
Shakespeare, William, 2, 7, 16, 46,
141, 152, 155, 163
Sherman, Stuart P., 161, 170n.1,
177n.1
Ship Money, 6
Shirley, James, 13, 58, 151, 154,
169n.29
Singleton, William, 168n.26
Spanish Gipsy, The, 10, 11, 168n.24
Staple of News, The, 23, 151,
167n.11; *see also* Jonson
Stavig, Mark, 49, 74, 97, 152, 167n.6,
169n.2, 170n.3, 172nn.6,10,
174n.11
Steiner, George, 173n.2
'Stella', Lady Rich, 9
Suckling, John, 8, 150, 176n.11
Sun's Darling, The, 10
Sydney, Sir Philip, 9
Sykes, H. Dugdale, 161, 168n.24,
179n.1
Swan Theatre, The, 4, 173n.14

'Tis Pity She's a Whore, 9, 12, 14, 35,
36-57, 59, 66, 73, 78, 83, 152, 154,
157, 158, 159, 164-5, 168-9n.27,
170n.1, 171n.1, 172n.5, 173n.16

Tomlinson, T. B., 159, 167n.4
Tourneur, Cyril, 56
*True and Wonderful History of
Perkin Warbeck*, 106; *see also*
Gainsford

Ure, Peter, 172n.8, 174n.7

Valentinian, 140; *see also* Beaumont
and Fletcher
Van Dyck, 6
Volpone, 131; *see also* Johnson

Webster, John, 11, 24, 55, 56, 63,
168n.23, 170n.3
White Devil, The, 63, 172n.4; *see
also* Webster
Wickham, Glynne, 167nn.8,12,13
Wild Duck, The, 137
Witch of Edmonton, The, 10, 11, 12,
117, 125, 133, 168n.24
Wits, The, 4; *see also* Davenant
Woman Killed with Kindness, A,
125, 126, 136, 159, 174n.7; *see
also* Heywood
Women Beware Women, 38, 54, 128,
130, 172n.9, 176n.4
Wood, Harvey, 170n.5